Sticky,
Chewy,
Messy, Gooey
Treats
FOR
Kids

CHRONICLE BOOKS

SAN FRANCISCO

Sticky, Chewy, Messy, Gooey Treats FOR Kids

By Jill O'Connor

Photographs by Leigh Beisch

Dedication

For my mother, with love, who continues to teach me so many things, without ever having to say a word.

Acknowledgments

Thank you to my editor, Bill LeBlond, who always makes the process of writing a book for Chronicle a pleasure and a delight, and to Amy Treadwell and Sarah Billingsley for all their help and kindness with my many questions and concerns. Thank you to Leigh Beisch and Katie Christ for their beautiful images and especially to Ayako Akazawa for her distinctive and lovely design, and to my copy editor, Carrie Bradley. You turned my simple manuscript pages into a beautiful book with a personality all its own. Many thanks to Karen Tack and Alan Richardson, author and photographer of the wonderful book *Hello Cupcake! Irresistibly Playful Creations Anyone Can Make*. Your recipe for Almost Homemade Vanilla Buttercream inspired my recipe for Pink Marshmallow Fluff Icing—great minds think alike! Thanks to Heather Nunnelly, recipe tester extraordinaire, for juggling your culinary school responsibilities while simultaneously testing every recipe in this book with humor, enthusiasm, and honesty—you saved my life on more than one occasion. To my friends and family who took so much of their time to test, taste, and tell me what they really thought about the recipes in this book—I could not have done it without you. A heartfelt "Thank you, you're fabulous!" goes out to: Bob and Carole Reek, the best parents. Ever. Seth and Veronica Reek and my nephew Ethan and niece Jillian, for their giddy enthusiasm for all things chocolate. Adam and Sandy Reek and my niece Ava, who, like her Auntie Jill, knows the pleasure of "Ah, food!" Pete and Deb O'Connor and my nephews, Brian and Matthew, who took their baking and tasting assignments very seriously. Nikki and John O'Connor and my nephews, Michael and Luc, who baked with me in spirit, if not in the kitchen. Valerie Lewis and Monica Holmes, the heart and soul of Hicklebee's Children's Books in San Jose, California, who—with their fabulous staff—have always been there to support and encourage me. Cheryl Sternman Rule, an excellent writer and lover of good food, and her sons, Alex and Andrew—my two favorite banana pancake men. Sandi Burke and her sons, Alex and Adam, get a medal for being brave and actually baking from scratch. Stephanie Galeckas, a wonderful baker, and her daughter, Emma, and son, Thomas, who mastered the art of Peanut Butter–Pretzel Bonbons and lived to tell the tale. Cambi Martin who helped me so much without ever having to turn on the stove, and to her son, Zack, and daughter, Alex, who know a good chocolate cake when they taste one. Lynell Sanchez and her daughter, Anissa, and son, Jose, who taught me so much about peanut allergies and introduced me to the charms of sun butter. Susan Farnworth, a fantastic cooking teacher and an enthusiastic expert about baking and cooking with children, and her daughter, Amy, and sons, Sam and Scott, for their enthusiasm in the kitchen. Shelly and Randy High, two great cooks and terrific foodies, and their son, Alex (who wins the unofficial French toast–eating contest). Kayla Vierra and her son, Joey, and sweet daughter, Grace, who baked and tasted chocolate chip cookies and gooey chocolate pudding with carefree abandon. Nella Henninger and her grandchildren, Miles and Hazel, who tested recipes together during their mountain vacation. Joel Bernard and Scott Maloney who ran across the Coronado Bay Bridge just to taste my New York, New York Super Crumb Cake and give me their verdict. Leah Karen Bentley and her daughters, Eliana and Jade, who made A Is For Apple Pie–Stuffed French Toast and ate it for dinner. Debbie Homeier and her daughter, Maddy, and son, Joey, for trying my recipes before we had even met. Nancie McDermott, who knows what it is like to survive the writing process. Denise Marchessault and her daughters, Lucie and Elise, my Canadian connection, who spread these recipes to her friends in Canada and England for testing, and sent me such great advice and excellent quotes. Chrissy Hee, Richard Rea, and Lou Martinez, culinary students who tapped into their inner child to help me test these recipes while in the middle of their final exams. Tracy Howell, the artistic leader of Brownie Troop 5145, and all the little Brownies who never tried to sugarcoat it, and always told me what they really thought: Sophia O'Connor, Emma Galeckas, Joie Nunnelly, Gemma Burrows, Taylor Seay, Eliana Bentley, Devynn Howell, Isabella Armstrong, Zoe Collins, Amy Schafer, and Lilly, Rose, and Daisy Cuthbert. And most of all to my husband, Jim, a real knight in shining armor—especially when I am battling my two demons—the computer and that devil procrastination—and to my two wonderful daughters, Olivia and Sophia, who are overjoyed to finally be welcomed into my kitchen and who make it a much livelier, and sweeter, place as a result.

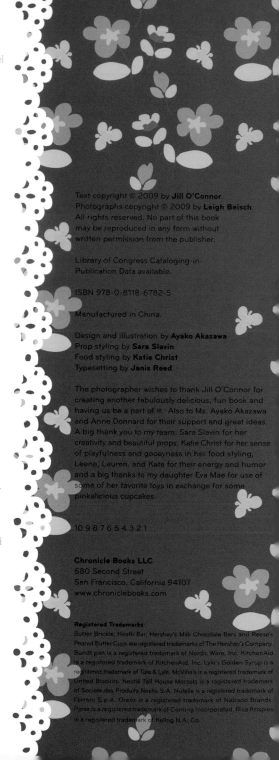

Library of Congress Cataloging-in-Publication Data available.

ISBN 978-0-8118-6782-5

Manufactured in China.

Design and illustration by **Ayako Akazawa**
Prop styling by **Sara Slavin**
Food styling by **Katie Christ**
Typesetting by **Janis Reed**

The photographer wishes to thank Jill O'Connor for creating another fabulously delicious, fun book and having us be a part of it. Also to Ms. Ayako Akazawa and Anne Donnard for their support and great ideas. A big thank you to my team: Sara Slavin for her creativity and beautiful props, Katie Christ for her sense of playfulness and gooeyness in her food styling, Leena, Lauren, and Kate for their energy and humor and a big thanks to my daughter Eva Mae for use of some of her favorite toys in exchange for some pinkalicious cupcakes.

10 9 8 7 6 5 4 3 2 1

Chronicle Books LLC
680 Second Street
San Francisco, California 94107
www.chroniclebooks.com

Introduction

I have a secret. Baking with children isn't always easy. I realized this a long time ago when I tried to make chocolate cupcakes with my daughter Sophia, an activity that ended badly with her running crying from the kitchen when I took the icing spatula away from her. My older daughter, Olivia, in all her teenage wisdom, likes to call me "mean chef." My husband sometimes pretends an invisible time clock is ticking (sound effects included) while I am trying to teach one of them to cook, to see just how many seconds I can stand it before I snatch the whisk from their fingers. Is it just another case of the cobbler's children having no shoes, or am I really just a big kitchen ogre?

When I was growing up, I spent a lot of time in the kitchen, and a lot of time thinking about food. When I was ten, I made my parents a pot roast dinner for their wedding anniversary, tucking carrots and potatoes around the meat and sprinkling it all with dried onion soup mix before cooking it. In Mrs. Laraway's fifth-grade class, I wrote my big class research report about chocolate; I wrapped the report cover in burlap and cut a big cacao pod out of brown construction paper and pasted it on the front. Very arty. To look for visual aids, my mother took me to Cost Plus World Market, which was very exotic to me at the time, and I found little chocolate-covered grasshoppers wrapped in silver candy paper. I fed them to the class at the end of my oral report and only after they had taken their last bite did I tell them what those crunchy bits were. At the time my point was that chocolate can make anything taste good. I quelled any possible rioting by passing out big Hershey's Milk Chocolate Bars before I sat down.

I don't have many memories of my mother actually *teaching* me to cook. She was, and still is, a great cook, and was always trying new recipes. She made jam every summer from the apricots that grew on the thirty trees in our backyard; she even tried her hand at homemade fruit leather, which was one of my brothers' and my favorite snacks.

There were always homemade cookies in the cookie jar, and during the Christmas holidays there was an extravaganza of candied nuts, fudge, chocolate chip–peppermint meringues, and a myriad selection of complicated new sweets that she experimented with every year. I watched my mother fill our house with good food, and she let me loose in the kitchen too, giving me free rein to experiment, or make a mess and discover things on my own. Now that I am a mother myself, I realize just how brave she really was. I know she was there, cooking herself, or maybe just making sure I was working safely, but what I realize now is that cooking was always a more solitary pursuit than a social one for me; it was a time to experiment and think, and to let my imagination run wild.

Now that my own children are showing an interest in cooking, how can I banish my inner Kitchen Witch—that inner perfectionist—and finally invite them into my domain? Most children love sweets, so I think a great way to start learning the basics of baking is by helping a little or just by watching someone bake something they love to eat. That is how *Sticky, Chewy, Messy, Gooey Treats for Kids* was born. I find that the trick is to make the treats special enough to grab the kids' attention, delicious enough to make it worth pulling out all the pots and pans for, and foolproof enough not to be ruined by anyone's less-than-perfect baking technique.

I have tried to make the recipes in this book simple with common pantry staples and with uncomplicated and easy to understand instructions that are stress-free for parents to make alone, or with their children. Some recipes are easy enough for children to prepare with just a little assistance from an adult, like the Matterhorn Mountain Shortbread Cookies, while others require more adult supervision as with the Down-Home Praline and Pumpkin Spice Donuts—kids can help mix the donut dough and cut them out with the donut cutter, while an adult handles the frying and glazing.

Banana Split Pancakes are delicious and easy breakfast treats that children can help stir together before an adult fries them in a heated griddle. Everyone can assemble their own breakfast "split"—topping their pancakes with fresh berries and bananas and a warm drizzle of Nutella (a chocolate-hazelnut spread invented in Italy that is gaining popularity here in the United States) or my easy butterscotch syrup that can be assembled in five minutes. Biscuits, scones, and the pastry for an old English favorite, jam roly-poly, are made with grated frozen butter—an easy technique that ensures flaky pastry every time you make it. Hunka Chunka Chewy Chocolate Chip Cookies require equipment no more complicated than a wooden spoon and a bowl to deliver jumbo cookies that one little girl told me tasted "as good as store-bought."

There are recipes here for sweets that both children and adults will love—cookies, cupcakes, biscuits, fruit crisps, and ice-cream treats—perfect for any time of day and for any occasion, from birthdays, holidays, church picnics, and potluck suppers to leisurely breakfasts and after-school snacks. There are recipes for fun and easy weeknight desserts that double as science projects, like Houdini's Hot Chocolate Pudding Cake; it goes into the oven a simple cake batter topped, oddly enough, with boiling water only to emerge a deliciously moist chocolate cake atop a gooey chocolate pudding–like sauce (made especially to be eaten next to a big scoop of vanilla ice cream). Where applicable, I have also included tips on essential techniques that are helpful for both beginning and seasoned bakers, like how to measure and sift flour, separate an egg, properly beat egg whites, and melt chocolate, or how to make the perfect crumble topping for an authentic New York crumb cake.

So grab your kids, some butter, sugar, a few eggs, and a little chocolate, and dig in! If your kitchen sometimes hides a kitchen ogre like mine does, pull out one of the recipes in this book and scare that meanie away for good.

Equipment

THE BIG STUFF

The following list includes electrical appliances that make baking and whipping up desserts a breeze.

BLENDER: This is perfect for blending and puréeing sauces, both sweet and savory.

ELECTRIC DEEP-FRYER: These are equipped with a thermometer that automatically controls the temperature of the oil as you fry. They eliminate any guesswork involved in the process and make frying perfect donuts easy.

ELECTRIC FRYING PAN: A high-sided electric frying pan can be used instead of a deep-fat fryer for donuts.

ELECTRIC GRIDDLE: Countertop electric griddles come in a variety of sizes that enable you to cook large batches of pancakes and bacon at one time. The temperature can be preset, ensuring perfectly cooked pancakes every time.

ELECTRIC HAND MIXER: This inexpensive kitchen essential with small, detachable beaters is necessary for mixing together most light cake batters, whipped cream, meringues, and soft cookie dough. A sturdy hand mixer is lightweight and convenient, and may be more suitable for mixing together smaller quantities of ingredients.

FOOD PROCESSOR: This kitchen counter workhorse is the perfect tool for quickly grinding nuts, bread, and cookie crumbs; puréeing fruit; and preparing some basic cake and cookie batters. It is the perfect choice for mixing doughs and batters that do not need to be heavily whipped and beaten.

STAND MIXER: In all my cookbooks, I recommend a large stand mixer—like a KitchenAid mixer. You can definitely live without one, but having one makes baking faster, simpler, and much more pleasant. This mixer makes recipes such as meringues, large batches of cookie dough, and homemade marshmallows much easier to tackle. With a paddle attachment for cookie, cake, and pastry doughs; a whisk attachment for beating heavy cream, meringue, and buttercream; and a dough hook to knead sweet and savory bread dough, a stand mixer is a godsend, and pays for itself many times over.

ESSENTIAL COOKWARE

The following tools and equipment will ensure the finest, most precise results every time you cook and bake.

CANDY/OIL THERMOMETER: Don't be afraid of recipes that call for a candy thermometer. These thermometers are made to measure the temperature of sugar syrups when making candy, and oil when deep-frying. They are easy to use, very accurate, and inexpensive. They clip onto the side of the pan and are essential for foolproof fudge, homemade marshmallows, toffees, and other candies, and for successfully monitoring the temperature of oil to ensure that donuts and other fried foods are light and crisp, not heavy or greasy.

ICE-CREAM SCOOP: These come in a variety of sizes. I find the standard 2-ounce scoop with a self-releasing spring-loaded scraper to be the most convenient for making perfectly proportioned scoops of cookie dough, for portioning out cupcake batter for perfectly even cupcakes, and, of course, for scooping ice cream.

NONSTICK GRIDDLE PAN: A flat, heavy, metal pan, usually with nonstick coating, for use on the stovetop. It is useful for cooking pancakes, French toast, and other savory dishes that need quick cooking on a flat surface.

NONSTICK SAUTÉ AND FRYING PANS: A nonstick 8-inch, 10-inch, or 12-inch sauté pan makes sticky jobs like sautéing French toast and cooking sliced apples much easier. Nonstick cookware prevents sticky foods from burning and sticking to the pan as they cook, and makes cleanup a breeze. Just be careful not to overheat the pan as you are cooking or use metal utensils as this can damage the coating.

OVEN THERMOMETER: This is an inexpensive necessity that will accurately assess the temperature of your oven; it prevents both over- and undercooking baked goods.

SAUCEPANS: Invest in a small set of straight-sided, heavy-duty stainless-steel saucepans in 1-quart, 2-quart, and 3-quart sizes with matching lids. A Dutch oven or stainless steel stockpot is also useful, and can be used for stovetop deep-fat frying.

ESSENTIAL BAKEWARE

Stock your cupboards with the following essentials, and you can make almost any dessert in this book, and beyond.

BUNDT PAN: The best models of this decorative tube pan are made of heavy cast aluminum and coated with a nonstick finish. The hole in the center of the pan facilitates faster, more even baking.

GLASS PIE DISH: These are usually made from heat-resistant Pyrex that can go from oven to freezer. Glass pie dishes make it easier to see how well your crust is browning.

MUFFIN PANS: Standard muffin pans have 12 cups and hold ¼ to ⅓ cup of batter each. Also available in mini-muffin cups or jumbo cups, which are sometimes called "Texas-size." Muffin pans with a nonstick coating make cleanup much easier.

PORCELAIN CUSTARD CUPS OR RAMEKINS: Ovenproof porcelain 2-ounce and 4-ounce ramekins and custard cups make perfect containers for individual servings of puddings, mousses, pot de crèmes, and ice cream.

RECTANGULAR BAKING PANS: Metal or ceramic pans measuring 9 by 13 inches and at least 2 to 2½ inches deep are the most versatile for sheet cakes, coffee cakes, brownies, and bar cookies.

ROUND CAKE PANS: Choose sturdy, good-quality aluminum cake pans. The most versatile are 8-inch or 9-inch round pans that are at least 2 inches deep. Purchase two of the same size for layer cakes.

SOUFFLÉ DISH: A 1- to 2-quart soufflé dish is a lovely choice for desserts other than a soufflé; small fruit crumbles and warm pudding cakes can be taken from oven to table in these dishes. Cold desserts like puddings and mousses can also be chilled and served from a soufflé dish.

SQUARE PANS: Metal or ceramic pans measuring 8 or 9 inches square and at least 2 to 2½ inches deep are the most versatile for smaller cakes, coffee cakes, bar cookies, and brownies.

TART PANS: These metal tart pans have shallow sides, a decorative fluted edge and a removable bottom, which makes it easy to remove the tart for a beautiful visual display. A 9-inch or 10-inch round pan is the most versatile, but they are also available in square and rectangle shapes and in smaller tartlet sizes for individual servings.

EVERYDAY TOOLS AND EQUIPMENT

No kitchen is complete without the following essential, and inexpensive, equipment.

BAKING SHEETS: Rimmed, aluminum half-sheet pans are durable and versatile; available in restaurant-supply and kitchenware shops, they are inexpensive and last forever. Insulated baking sheets, made by sandwiching two sheets of metal together with a cushion of air between them, are perfect for baking delicate cookies and pastries that you do not want to burn or brown excessively. Two half-sheet pans and one insulated baking sheet make for a good start.

BOWLS: Stainless-steel bowls are lightweight, inexpensive, and very durable. They do not react with acidic ingredients and come in a variety of sizes. Tempered glass bowls, especially a set of nesting bowls, are a great investment. The variety of sizes makes them versatile, and unlike stainless-steel bowls, they can go in the microwave for melting butter or chocolate.

BOX GRATER: This old-fashioned, heavy-duty metal shredder has four sides, each with a different cutting surface. One side has large holes with sharp edges; typically used to grate cheese, it is also perfect for grating frozen butter.

COOLING RACKS: Choose one or two sturdy, rectangular metal wire racks with slightly raised feet. Cooling cakes and cookies on a rack allows air to circulate around them, cooling them faster and eliminating the chance of a soggy bottom.

KNIVES: Every beginner should start with three basic knives: a 10-inch chef's knife, a paring knife, and a serrated knife. Remember, you get what you pay for; purchase knives that are heavy-duty, sturdy, and well made for lasting quality and durability.

MEASURING CUPS: You will need both liquid and dry measuring cups. Liquid measuring cups have a handle and a pouring spout and are usually made of glass or clear plastic with the measurements for ounces and cups printed on the side of the cup. Dry measuring cups come in sets of graduated sizes: ¼ cup, ^{1}/$_3$ cup, ½ cup, and 1 cup. I like stainless-steel cups with a straight, flat rim for easy leveling.

MEASURING SPOONS: These come in sets of spoons in increments of ¼ teaspoon, ½ teaspoon, 1 teaspoon, and 1 tablespoon. Sturdy stainless-steel spoons are the most durable.

MESH SIEVE: This is my choice for sifting and aerating dry ingredients together. Add the ingredients to the sieve and place over a large bowl. Simply tap the sides of the sieve with the palm of your hand to move the ingredients into the waiting bowl underneath. Sieves can also be used to strain custards and sauces.

Ingredients

PAPER MUFFIN LINERS: Paper liners add a festive touch to your cupcakes and muffins, but they also insulate them from the intense heat of the oven and help to keep them moister, longer.

PARCHMENT PAPER: This nonstick paper used for lining cake pans and baking sheets comes in a roll and is usually available next to the foil in grocery stores.

RUBBER OR SILICONE SPATULAS: Heatproof silicone is an improvement over the more old-fashioned rubber spatula. It won't stain or absorb flavors and can withstand higher temperatures. Use these spatulas to efficiently fold ingredients together and for scraping batters out of bowls.

WIRE WHISKS: Whisks come in all sizes and shapes from fat, round *balloon whisks* for whipping egg whites and cream, to longer, narrower whisks with stiffer wires called *piano whisks* that are used for beating heavier ingredients together and preventing lumps from forming in cooked custards and sauces. Purchasing one of each is a good start.

WOODEN SPOONS: Every kitchen needs a big crock of wooden spoons on the counter. They are sturdy, inexpensive, and long lasting; they will not scrape or damage your pots and pans, and the handle remains cool in your hand when stirring the hottest sauces, caramels, custards, and puddings.

"Ah, food!" Ava Reek, age 18 months

BUTTER: There is nothing like real butter and there is no substitute. Most professional bakers prefer the taste of unsalted butter in their baking, and I am no exception. Unsalted butter makes it easier to control the salt content in your recipe and usually tastes fresher than salted butter. That said, time will not stand still and the earth will not swallow you whole if you use salted butter in any of these recipes. If you do, take care with the added salt, and proceed with caution.

CHOCOLATE CHIPS: I tried to keep the recipes, and their ingredients, in this book as simple as possible, and used real, semisweet chocolate chips for the recipes using melted chocolate as one of the ingredients. I prefer Nestlé Toll House Morsels, and used them when testing these recipes. If you would like to use another chocolate in your recipes, make sure to use one with no more than 56 percent cacao, as anything stronger may be too bittersweet.

CONFECTIONERY COATING: Sometimes called summer coating, candy coating, or wafer chocolate, confectionery coating is used for making candy molds and for dipping small candies and bonbons. Because it does not require tempering like chocolate, confectionery coating is sturdier and less temperamental to work with and is a good choice for beginning candy makers. Confectionery coating is available in white, milk, and dark chocolate flavors, as well as in a variety of pastels and vivid colors.

DAIRY: Unless otherwise stated in the recipe, use the dairy product listed in the ingredient list. Whole milk, half-and-half, and heavy cream deliver a different taste and "mouth feel" to the recipes. Do not substitute nonfat milk or soy products, as there may be a difference in taste and texture to the final dessert.

EGGS: Use large eggs for the best results in these recipes. Large eggs weigh about 2 ounces each.

FLOUR: I use two kinds of flour for most of the recipes in this book:

ALL-PURPOSE FLOUR (bleached and unbleached): Most of the recipes in this book call for all-purpose flour. All-purpose flour is milled with a mixture of hard and soft wheat and contains 10 to 12 percent protein. It is useful for most cookies, sturdy cakes, pancakes, scones, donuts, and other pastries and baked goods that call for a lot of moisture-enriching ingredients such as sour cream, heavy cream, and butter.

CAKE FLOUR: Cake flour is soft and fine textured. It has a lower protein content than all-purpose flour, 6 to 8 percent. Cake flour is bleached and low in gluten with a smooth, almost silky and creamy quality. It is an excellent choice for delicate fine-textured cakes and delivers a particularly velvety crumb.

FROZEN BERRIES: I use frozen berries to make fruit purées and for sauces and jams in this book. Frozen berries are a wonderful substitute for fresh in these recipes. Berries that are completely ripe and ready to eat, but are too ripe for shipping fresh to market, are often used for IQF (instant quick freeze) berries. These ripe berries are flash frozen and packed, unsweetened. They are perfect for making flavorful sauces and jams when thawed, puréed, and sieved.

HONEY: I used mild-flavored honey like clover or orange blossom to add sweetness, moisture, and a mild honey flavor to my recipes. Stronger honeys may compete with the other flavors in the recipe. In general, the lighter in color the honey, the milder its flavor will be.

LYLE'S GOLDEN SYRUP: This golden, all-natural sugarcane syrup is similar in viscosity to corn syrup, but is distinguished by its rich, caramel-like, almost buttery flavor and aroma. Golden syrup is a delicious staple in British baking, and is worth seeking out in the United States. It is available in larger grocery stores and specialty food markets and from on-line sources.

MARSHMALLOW FLUFF: A trademarked sweet produced in Massachusetts, this is one of my favorite sweet ingredients. Although it is becoming easier to find in the western United States, it is a staple in the East. You can also order it straight from the company—they are happy to ship it anywhere in the world.

NUTS: Purchase shelled nut halves and toast and chop them yourself for the freshest flavor. Store nuts in the freezer to prolong their shelf life and prevent them from going rancid. Double-bag them to prevent freezer burn.

OATMEAL: Oatmeal adds a sweet, nutty flavor to cookies and crumbles. I use old-fashioned rolled oats in cookies for their wonderful texture and chewiness, but in crisps and crumbles, I prefer quick-cooking oats—they have the same sweet, nutty flavor, but are more delicate in texture so as not to overwhelm the fruit fillings.

Success Made Simple

PEANUT BUTTER: I use traditional creamy peanut butter in the recipes. Do not use natural peanut butter, as the texture is not the same and the recipe will suffer.

SUGAR: Look for "pure cane sugar" on the label when buying sugar for baking. I use pure cane granulated, super-fine (sometimes labeled "baker's sugar"), confectioners', light and dark brown, and raw sugars in the recipes in this book. If the label does not say "pure cane sugar," you could be purchasing sugar made from sugar beets. Although chemically the same, many bakers and pastry chefs find the flavor and texture of desserts made with cane sugar superior to those made with beet sugar, especially for recipes requiring caramelizing, such as caramel sauce and butterscotch.

SUN BUTTER: Sun butter is a savory spread made with sunflower seeds. Sun butter has the same creamy texture of peanut butter, but because it is made with a seed instead of a nut, is appropriate to use in recipes for people with peanut and other tree nut allergies. Sun butter can be substituted in equal proportions in most recipes calling for peanut butter.

"Mom, you know I don't read directions—I skim."
Olivia O'Connor, age 15, disobeying the first rule for baking success

READ THE RECIPE: Make sure you read the recipe completely before you start baking, to ensure that you have all the ingredients and equipment you need, and that you understand the time required to prepare the dish.

GET ORGANIZED: Before you start cooking, assemble your ingredients. Make sure ingredients like butter are removed from the refrigerator and given enough time to come to room temperature. You can even measure ingredients into individual bowls before you begin. This is a good idea when baking with children—it makes them feel like a TV chef, and ensures that no eggshells accidentally fall into the batter or that too much salt is added to the cookie dough.

MEASURE CORRECTLY: Baking is as much a science as an art, so make sure to measure your ingredients correctly. Measure liquids in liquid measuring cups and dry ingredients in flat-edged measuring cups.

NO SUBSTITUTIONS: Before you start substituting or eliminating ingredients, make the recipe the way it is originally written first. This will give you an idea about how it is supposed to look and taste. Drastically reducing ingredients like sugar and butter, or eliminating egg yolks can change not only the taste, but the texture of cakes, cookies, and other baked goods as well.

TAKE YOUR TIME: When baking, there is no need to rush. Take your time to read the recipe completely and follow the instructions carefully. You will be pleasantly surprised with the fruits of your labor!

1

What's Your Story, Morning Glory?

Breakfast Sweets to Make You Rise and Shine

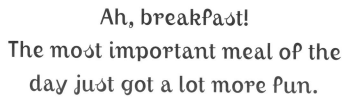

Ah, breakfast!
The most important meal of the
day just got a lot more fun.

No more cold bowls of cereal or lonely plates of plain scrambled eggs.
Everyone will come running to the table to sample the recipes in this chapter.
How about waking up to a warm plate of tender, homemade pancakes piled
high with fresh strawberries and ripe bananas and dripping with a buttery syrup
made from brown sugar; or crisp fingers of toast spread with butter and cinnamon
sugar ready for dipping in a cool cup of applesauce; or velvety scones warm
from the oven slathered with a surprisingly simple, homemade berry jam?
A special breakfast doesn't have to be complicated or difficult to prepare;
I have developed morning specialties easily made by one person, or with a whole
family pitching in to help. There are simple tasks a preschooler can help with, from
peeling apples and stirring together cinnamon sugar, to more complicated
assignments like rolling jam up into a flaky pastry for warm Strawberry Jam
Roly-Poly, or cutting out and frying up homemade donuts, rich with pumpkin
and warm spices and glazed with a sweet praline icing, which require
just a little more experience in the kitchen.
So roll up your sleeves, tie on your apron, and dig in. There are
recipes in this chapter to tempt everyone's taste buds and give
everyone in your family a reason to wake up and walk
out the front door with a big smile
on their face.

Mmmm—sweet and snow white, with a refreshing bite of peppermint, this belly-warming drink will satisfy all white chocolate lovers. Served with a candy cane swizzle stick, this hot chocolate becomes the perfect Christmas drink to sip beside a warm fire. But why stop at Christmas? For your Valentine, tint the drink rose-petal pink, trade the peppermint for a few drops of vanilla, and top with a pink-streaked billow of whipped cream. To celebrate Saint Patrick's Day, swap green food coloring for the pink, top with a green-tinted homemade marshmallow (page 83), and scatter with shamrock-shaped sprinkles. The possibilities are endless.

Pepperminty Wintery White Hot Chocolate SERVES 4

4 CUPS WHOLE MILK

1 POUND WHITE CHOCOLATE, FINELY CHOPPED

2 TEASPOONS PEPPERMINT EXTRACT

PINCH OF SALT

4 PEPPERMINT CANDY CANES (UNWRAPPED) FOR STIRRING

IN A MEDIUM SAUCEPAN OVER MEDIUM HEAT, warm the milk until it is very hot and just about to boil (but do not boil). Remove from the heat and whisk in the chocolate, peppermint extract, and salt until the chocolate is completely melted and combined with the milk. For a fluffier drink, pour the mixture into a blender and purée on high for a few seconds before serving. Pour into cups and serve with a candy cane for stirring.

My daughter Sophia has a passion for cinnamon toast; she loves it for breakfast or as a snack before bedtime, cut into bite-size squares (crusts removed, of course). It was the first sweet I ever learned to make for myself, and it is still one of my favorite comfort foods even surrounded by more exotic or fancy fare. What could be nicer than a crisp, buttery slab of toast spread with a thick blanket of cinnamon-spiked sugar, warm and melting like a gooey, granular icing into all the nooks and crannies? Simple perfection, made all the more so when cut into slim fingers for dipping into a cup of homemade applesauce.

Cinnamon Toast Soldiers with Mostly McIntosh Sauce

SERVES 4 TO 6

½ CUP GRANULATED SUGAR

2 TEASPOONS GROUND CINNAMON

6 SLICES FIRM-TEXTURED WHITE OR WHOLE-GRAIN BREAD

UNSALTED BUTTER, AT ROOM TEMPERATURE

MOSTLY MCINTOSH SAUCE (FACING PAGE)

IN A SMALL BOWL, mix the sugar and cinnamon together. Toast the bread until it is very crisp and brown on both sides. Spread each slice with very soft butter until the butter melts into the hot toast. Sprinkle each slice of toast with 1 table-spoon of the cinnamon-sugar mixture. Shake off any excess sugar that doesn't stick to the butter. Cut the crusts from the toast and cut each slice lengthwise into two or three long fingers. Serve the toast warm with a dish of cool McIntosh sauce on the side for dipping.

The smell of buttered toast simply talked to Toad, and with no uncertain voice; talked of warm kitchens, of breakfasts on frosty mornings, of cozy parlour firesides on winter evenings . . .
from The Wind in the Willows, *by Kenneth Grahame*

Perfect English Soldiers

Toast soldiers are icons of the British breakfast table. Cut thin, and toasted until very crisp, they are usually served buttered and ready to dip into the warm yolk of a soft-boiled egg. Why they are called soldiers is anybody's guess, but I think it is because they are meant to be served crisp and ramrod straight—no wimpy, slouching, soggy soldiers allowed! The ideal width for a proper toast soldier is apparently 22 millimeters (about 7/8 inch), the perfect fit for dipping into the center of your egg (or your ramekin of applesauce).

Mostly McIntosh Sauce

MAKES 2 1/2 TO 3 CUPS

McIntosh apples are a favorite for sauces—their sweet, tender flesh cooks down to a fine sauce. I like to add a few crisp, green Granny Smith apples to the mix to give the finished sauce an underlying tart and sassy kick. Grating the Granny Smith apples before adding them to the McIntosh apples helps them to cook faster and blend smoothly into the finished sauce.

5 McINTOSH APPLES, PEELED, CORED, AND THINLY SLICED

2 GRANNY SMITH APPLES, PEELED, CORED, AND COARSELY GRATED

JUICE OF 1/2 LEMON (ABOUT 3 TABLESPOONS)

1/2 TO 3/4 CUP GRANULATED SUGAR

1/4 CUP WATER

1/2 TO 1 TEASPOON GROUND CINNAMON (OPTIONAL)

IN A LARGE, heavy-bottomed saucepan over medium-low heat, combine the sliced and grated apples, the lemon juice, 1/2 cup of the sugar, and the water. Cover and cook, stirring occasionally, until the apples start to soften and the sugar dissolves, about 30 minutes. Taste the sauce for sweetness. If a sweeter sauce is desired, stir in up to 1/4 cup sugar, a tablespoon at a time. Stir in the cinnamon (if using) to taste and continue cooking until the apples have cooked down into a fine sauce, 20 to 30 minutes longer. Remove from the heat and let cool completely. The applesauce can be covered and refrigerated for up to 4 days.

Sunday breakfast is a fun meal for kids to help prepare. The mood is bright and everyone is relaxed and ready to pitch in. These sweet, fragrant pancakes are a festive choice, piled high with fresh strawberries and sliced bananas and smothered in gooey, chocolaty Nutella or Buttery Brown Sugar Syrup. The kids can help mash the banana and measure out the simple ingredients for the batter before an adult cooks the pancakes on the hot griddle. Although perfect for a leisurely weekend breakfast, they really are a snap to prepare and (when all the planets are properly aligned) can even be whipped up on a weekday morning. Make sure your bananas are very ripe—really overripe—for the sweetest, most tender pancakes.

Banana Split Pancakes

MAKES 9 OR 10 PANCAKES

1 LARGE EGG

1 CUP BUTTERMILK

2 TABLESPOONS UNSALTED BUTTER, MELTED

½ CUP MASHED VERY RIPE BANANA

1 TABLESPOON GRANULATED SUGAR

1 CUP ALL-PURPOSE FLOUR

1 TEASPOON BAKING POWDER

½ TEASPOON BAKING SODA

½ TEASPOON SALT

LARGE PINCH OF GROUND NUTMEG

OIL FOR BRUSHING THE PAN

MELTED BUTTER, SLICED FRESH BANANA, SLICED FRESH STRAW-BERRIES, WARMED NUTELLA, AND BUTTERY BROWN SUGAR SYRUP (PAGE 22) FOR SERVING

IN A MEDIUM BOWL, whisk together the egg, buttermilk, butter, banana, and sugar. In a separate bowl, sift together the flour, baking powder, baking soda, salt, and nutmeg.

POUR THE LIQUID INGREDIENTS OVER THE DRY INGREDIENTS AND STIR TOGETHER WITH A fork or small whisk just to combine (overstirring makes the pancakes tough). It is okay if the batter is a little bit lumpy.

HEAT A NONSTICK GRIDDLE OR SKILLET OVER MEDIUM-HIGH HEAT. Brush the pan lightly with oil and drop the batter onto the heated skillet in mounded ¼-cup portions. Cook the pancakes until the batter starts to brown around the edges and little bubbles start to form over the surface of the batter, 1 to 2 minutes. Use your spatula to lift a corner of the pancake to see if it is brown and lacy and ready to turn. Flip the pancake and finish cooking, 1 to 2 minutes longer. Repeat with the remaining pancake batter, brushing the pan with more oil when needed to prevent sticking.

SERVE THE WARM PANCAKES DRIZZLED WITH MELTED BUTTER, sliced bananas, fresh strawberries, warmed Nutella, and/or Buttery Brown Sugar Syrup.

"They're definitely not plain . . ."
Andrew Rule, age 8, eyeing his banana pancakes piled high with fruit and drizzled with Nutella

Going Bananas

When is a banana ripe enough? Bananas that are ripe enough to cook and bake with are usually way too ripe to consider eating. The fruit should be very soft, and the yellow skin should be more than just speckled with brown spots—almost completely brown—to ensure the deepest, sweetest banana flavor.

Flour Power

What's the best way to store and measure flour? I like to store my all-purpose flour in a large-mouthed glass canister. It's easy to see when I am running low, and the large opening in the canister makes measuring less messy and less complicated.

1   Before measuring, stir the flour to lighten it a little, as it tends to settle and become compacted.

2   Spoon the flour into the measuring cup, but do not shake the cup to settle or level it—you could end up with more flour than you need if you do.

3   Use the back of a knife and quickly level the top of the flour scraping the excess back into the container.

Buttery Brown Sugar Syrup

MAKES 1 CUP

1 CUP FIRMLY PACKED LIGHT BROWN SUGAR

2 TABLESPOONS UNSALTED BUTTER

½ CUP WATER

IN A MEDIUM SAUCEPAN OVER MEDIUM HEAT, combine all the ingredients. Swirl the pan occasionally to combine ingredients. When the butter is melted and the sugar is dissolved, increase the heat to high and bring the mixture to a boil. Reduce the heat to medium-low and simmer until the syrup thickens and is the consistency of warm maple syrup, about 6 to 8 minutes. Let cool slightly and serve. The syrup will continue to thicken as it cools.

Does the thought of preparing homemade jam make you want to lie down on the couch with a cold cloth over your eyes? Don't despair! Using frozen, organic, unsweetened berries enables you to make this quick and very easy berry jam any time of year in about 15 minutes. Frozen berries are actually a fine substitute for fresh, as they are usually picked at their peak of ripeness and frozen immediately. They are often riper than fresh fruits. Be sure to purchase fruit that is packed and frozen without sugar. Made without added pectin, this jam will set to a "soft gel," meaning it will be very thick and spreadable, but not as firm or gelatinous as store-bought jam or preserves. This jam will keep, tightly covered in the refrigerator, for up to 3 weeks.

Jumbled Berry Jam

MAKES 2 PINTS

1 BAG (10 OUNCES) FROZEN ORGANIC STRAWBERRIES

1 BAG (10 OUNCES) FROZEN ORGANIC BLACKBERRIES

1 BAG (10 OUNCES) FROZEN ORGANIC RASPBERRIES

JUICE OF ½ LEMON (ABOUT 1 TABLESPOON)

3 CUPS GRANULATED SUGAR

CHILL A SMALL PLATE IN THE FREEZER AND KEEP IT THERE, at the ready, to test the jam for proper jelling.

THAW THE FRUIT COMPLETELY. Combine the fruit and any accumulated juices, along with the lemon juice in a large saucepan or stockpot over medium heat. Cook just to heat through and, using a potato masher, coarsely crush most of the fruit. Add the sugar and increase the heat to high. Bring the mixture to a boil. Cook the fruit, stirring constantly, for 8 to 10 minutes. To test, put a spoonful of the jam on the chilled plate and leave it to sit for a few minutes. The jam is ready when it is thickened and firm enough to hold its shape on the plate without running or becoming watery, and your finger leaves a clean trail on the plate when pulled through the center of the jam. Spoon the jam into two 1-pint containers, cover tightly, and refrigerate until ready to use.

Jam on biscuits, jam on toast,
Jam is the thing that I like most.
Jam is sticky, jam is sweet,
Jam is tasty, jam's a treat—
Raspberry, strawberry, gooseberry, I'm very
FOND . . . OF . . . JAM!
from Bread and Jam for Frances, *by Russell Hoban*

I grew up reading plenty of children's books set in England. From *The Wolves of Willoughby Chase* and *Blackhearts in Battersea* to *The Secret Garden*, *The Chronicles of Narnia*, and every book ever written by Roald Dahl. Along with fantastical creatures, brave orphans, and the prerequisite sinister governess or head mistress, every book indulged in lavish descriptions of delicious food, conjuring images of cozy nurseries, nannies, and elaborate tea trays piled high with treacle tarts, gooseberry fools, and sturdy scones slathered with jam and thick cream. One of my favorite desserts is jam roly-poly. It is deliciously simple, and reminds me of a much larger version of the little jam pastries I made with leftover pie dough when I was young. The pastry here is a cross between a tender biscuit and flaky pie dough. A true, English roly-poly is made with suet and steamed, but this modern spin on the old classic is baked—delivering a crisp, tender-but-flaky pastry barely encasing the warm, bubbling strawberry jam inside. Serve warm wedges for breakfast sprinkled with confectioners' sugar, or for dessert with a big scoop of vanilla ice cream snuggling beside it.

Holy Moly! Strawberry Jam Roly-Poly SERVES 6

2 CUPS ALL-PURPOSE FLOUR

2 TEASPOONS BAKING POWDER

½ TEASPOON SALT

2 TABLESPOONS GRANULATED SUGAR, PLUS MORE FOR SPRINKLING

10 TABLESPOONS (1¼ STICKS) UNSALTED BUTTER, FROZEN

⅔ CUP (OR MORE IF NEEDED) ICE WATER

¾ CUP STRAWBERRY JAM (OR SUBSTITUTE RASPBERRY JAM, CHERRY PRESERVES, OR JUMBLED BERRY JAM, PAGE 23)

1 TABLESPOON WHOLE MILK FOR BRUSHING

LINE A BAKING SHEET WITH PARCHMENT PAPER. Preheat the oven to 400°F.

IN A MEDIUM BOWL, sift together the flour, baking powder, salt, and 2 tablespoons sugar. Set aside.

USING THE LARGE HOLES OF A BOX GRATER, grate the frozen butter into the flour mixture. Using your hands, lightly toss the flour and butter together. If the butter starts to soften, pop the mixture into the freezer for about 5 minutes to allow the butter to harden.

STIR ENOUGH ICE WATER INTO THE FLOUR AND BUTTER MIXTURE TO FORM A SOFT, shaggy dough that comes together to form a loose ball. If dough is too dry, add more ice water by tablespoons.

TRANSFER THE DOUGH ONTO A LIGHTLY FLOURED BOARD, gently kneading it just to combine (5 or 6 turns), but not allowing the butter to melt.

RUB A ROLLING PIN WITH FLOUR AND, on a flat surface lightly sprinkled with flour, roll the dough quickly into an approximately 9-by-13-inch rectangle.

CONTINUED

Pastry Perfection

Why do we sift the flour? Sifting the flour and other dry ingredients together ensures that everything is evenly combined. It also *aerates* the mixture, which just means air is incorporated into the particles of flour helping to make the pastry much lighter in texture.

Why is the butter frozen? Frozen butter is easier to grate, like cheese. Grating the butter is an easy way to ensure that small, even pieces of butter are distributed throughout the dough. When the pastry bakes, these little pieces of hard butter will melt, forming air pockets that make the pastry light, crisp, and flaky. Butter is easy to grate, even for little fingers, but as the butter gets smaller, it can get slippery, so have your child give the last bit of butter to you or a more experienced baker to finish grating.

Holy Moly! Strawberry Jam Roly-Poly

CONTINUED

SPREAD 4 OR 5 TABLESPOONS JAM OVER THE SURFACE OF THE DOUGH, leaving a 1-inch border on all sides. Starting from one long end, roll up the pastry like a jelly roll, brushing excess flour off the pastry as you go.

SEAL THE END SEAM WITH A LITTLE WATER AND TIGHTLY PINCH THE ENDS TO PREVENT THE JAM from seeping out. Place the pastry, seam side down, on the prepared baking sheet. Brush lightly with milk and sprinkle liberally with granulated sugar.

BAKE UNTIL THE PASTRY IS PUFFED AND GOLDEN BROWN, and little rivulets of jam are bubbling out the ends, about 30 minutes. Let cool briefly on the baking sheet and slice into 6 portions using a serrated knife. Warm the reserved jam in a small saucepan, or in a bowl heated in the microwave, and drizzle over slices of the pastry, if desired.

"Sifting is jolly hard work . . ."
Catie Bass, age 7,
baking with her mother

These are the tastiest scones I have ever eaten. Helen of Troy's face may have launched a thousand ships, but one taste of my friend Heather Nunnelly's tender and delicately sweet cream scones can make grown men go weak. A generous portion of butter for a flaky texture and heavy cream for a rich, velvety crumb is her secret. I've left their flavor pristine here, with the merest hint of vanilla, but you can doll them up with ½ cup of dried currants and a teaspoon or two of freshly grated lemon zest for a classic English treat.

Practically-Perfect-in-Every-Way Cream Scones MAKES 8 LARGE SCONES

3 CUPS ALL-PURPOSE FLOUR

6 TABLESPOONS GRANULATED SUGAR, PLUS MORE FOR SPRINKLING SCONES

1 TEASPOON SALT

4 ½ TEASPOONS BAKING POWDER

½ CUP (1 STICK) UNSALTED BUTTER, FROZEN

1 ⅓ CUPS COLD HEAVY CREAM, PLUS MORE FOR BRUSHING SCONES

1 TEASPOON PURE VANILLA EXTRACT

HONEY BUTTER (RECIPE FOLLOWS) FOR SERVING (OPTIONAL)

JUMBLED BERRY JAM (PAGE 23) FOR SERVING (OPTIONAL)

PREHEAT THE OVEN TO 400°F. Line a baking sheet with parchment paper or coat lightly with nonstick cooking spray.

SIFT THE FLOUR, sugar, salt, and baking powder into a medium bowl.

GRATE THE FROZEN BUTTER USING THE LARGE HOLES ON A BOX GRATER. Toss the butter with the dry ingredients. Make a well in the center of the flour mixture and pour in the cream and vanilla. Use a fork to gently pull the flour into the cream just until combined. Be careful not to overmix, or the final scones will be tough.

ONCE THE INGREDIENTS ARE COMBINED, turn the mixture out onto a lightly floured work surface. Turn the dough, fold it over on itself once or twice, and form the dough into a ball. Gently pat with your hands or use a rolling pin to roll the dough into a round that is about 8 inches in diameter and ½ inch thick.

CUT THE DOUGH IN HALF AND THEN INTO QUARTERS. Cut each quarter in half again, for 8 triangular scones. Place the scones on the prepared baking sheet at least 2 inches apart. Brush the tops of the scones lightly with cream and sprinkle liberally with sugar.

BAKE THE SCONES UNTIL THEY HAVE RISEN AND ARE A RICH, golden brown, 15 to 18 minutes. Remove from the oven and let cool slightly before serving. Serve with Honey Butter (recipe follows) or Jumbled Berry Jam (page 23, if using).

Honey Butter MAKES 1 CUP

½ CUP (1 STICK) UNSALTED BUTTER, AT ROOM TEMPERATURE

⅓ CUP MILD HONEY

¼ TEASPOON PURE VANILLA EXTRACT

PLACE THE SOFTENED BUTTER IN A MEDIUM BOWL AND SLOWLY DRIZZLE IN THE HONEY, beating briskly with a wooden spoon, to form a thick, creamy emulsion. Beat in the vanilla. Spoon the honey butter into a small dish and serve with warm scones.

New Yorkers are passionate about many things, but who knew crumb cake was one of them? Crumb cake traveled to America first with the Dutch and later with German immigrants, famous for their baking, sometime around the late 1800s. Its popularity spread among bakeries and home cooks alike. Now a favorite in the Big Apple, most bakeries, delis, coffee shops, and corner grocers sell large chunks of this buttery yellow cake topped with a generous heap of crisp, nubbled, brown sugar crumble. The trick to making the perfect crumb cake? Lots and lots of crumbs! Some versions have twice as much rocky crumble as cake, but I think the perfect recipe is an equal proportion of both, scattering the crumble thick and deep in moist chunks across the surface of the batter.

New York, New York Super Crumb Cake

MAKES ONE 9-BY-13-INCH CAKE

CRUMBLE

2 CUPS DARK BROWN SUGAR

2¼ CUPS ALL-PURPOSE FLOUR

1 TEASPOON GROUND CINNAMON

¼ TEASPOON SALT

1 CUP (2 STICKS) UNSALTED BUTTER, MELTED

CAKE BATTER

¾ CUP (1½ STICKS) UNSALTED BUTTER

1 CUP GRANULATED SUGAR

2 LARGE EGGS

2 TEASPOONS PURE VANILLA EXTRACT

1 CUP SOUR CREAM

2 CUPS ALL-PURPOSE FLOUR

1¼ TEASPOONS BAKING POWDER

½ TEASPOON BAKING SODA

¾ TEASPOON SALT

CONFECTIONERS' SUGAR FOR SPRINKLING

PREHEAT THE OVEN TO 350°F. Coat a 9-by-13-inch baking pan with nonstick cooking spray.

TO PREPARE THE CRUMBLE: In a medium bowl, stir together the brown sugar, flour, cinnamon, and salt until well combined. Add the melted butter and stir with a fork until the butter is completely combined and the mixture forms large, moist clumps. Set aside.

TO PREPARE THE BATTER: In a large bowl, beat the butter and sugar together with a hand mixer set at medium-high speed until light and fluffy, 3 to 4 minutes. Add the eggs, one at a time, beating just until well combined. Beat in the vanilla and sour cream. Sift together the flour, baking powder, baking soda, and salt. Fold the flour mixture into the batter by hand using a large rubber spatula.

SPREAD THE BATTER EVENLY INTO THE PREPARED PAN. Use your hands to sprinkle the crumble over the batter, making sure some of the larger clumps remain as you go. Cover the batter completely with crumble.

BAKE UNTIL A SKEWER INSERTED INTO THE CENTER OF THE CAKE COMES OUT CLEAN, and the crumble is slightly crisp, 30 to 35 minutes. Let cool on a wire rack for 10 to 15 minutes. Sprinkle with confectioners' sugar, cut into 15 squares, and serve.

"When I grow up, I want to be a baker and the weather girl."
Emma Galeckas, age 7, contemplating her future career path

The kitchen is my favorite room.
It's easy to keep clean.
I have a secret recipe for toasted tangerine.
from Moss Pillows, *by Rosemary Wells*

Quintessential Crumble

Melting the butter makes the perfect crumble: Melting the butter makes this streusel-like topping moist and slightly heavy, guaranteeing the large, rocky crumble that gives New York, New York Super Crumb Cake its star power. After mixing the flour, brown sugar, and butter together, allow the crumble to sit for a few minutes to continue to absorb the butter. As it sits, the crumble will start to solidify, so when the time comes to scatter it over the batter, you will be able to break it with your hands into small pebbles and larger, knobby chunks, ensuring your crumb cake's delicious authenticity.

Hey, Mr. Science!

What do baking powder and baking soda do? These ingredients are chemical leavening agents. That means they help baked goods rise and create a light and delicate texture in cakes, cookies, biscuits, and quick breads. Baking powder and baking soda expand the air bubbles already present in a batter; air bubbles are beaten in when eggs are whipped or when butter and sugar are creamed together. Baking soda needs an acid in the batter to really work well. Acidic ingredients include sour cream, yogurt, citrus juices, natural (not Dutch-processed) cocoa powder, molasses, and brown sugar. Baking soda also starts to work as soon as it comes into contact with the wet ingredients in the batter, therefore it needs to go into the oven as quickly as possible before its leavening "oomph" starts to fade. Baking powder is a combination of baking soda and an acid, like cream of tartar. It is considered "double-acting," which means it works twice—once when it hits the wet ingredients and again when it meets the heat of the oven. Sometimes recipes include both baking powder and baking soda; usually these batters contain a large amount of acidic ingredients like sour cream. The baking soda balances the acidity of the batter and helps make the final cake tender, and the baking powder helps the batter rise when it is baked.

Butterscotch, a delicious combination of butter and brown sugar, is the perfect complement to this rich, almost bread pudding–like French toast. This gooey, decadent treat is made to be enjoyed during a lazy weekend brunch with lots of crispy bacon on the side—the lush sweetness of the French toast and the crisp saltiness of the bacon is a flavor combination not to be missed. It is also very easy to prepare, and if you use a nonstick skillet, just as easy to clean up. One of my taste-testers, a strapping 17-year-old football player, ate 5 slices at once for breakfast. Make sure you have lots of vigorous activity planned like hiking, biking, or perhaps a quick sprint up Mt. Fuji to keep any guilty feelings at bay after digging into this truly decadent treat. Always have a bowl of ice water ready on the counter when working with hot sugar. If fingers get splashed with the hot syrup, immediately cool them down by plunging them into the cold water. Never use metal utensils when cooking with nonstick pans. Use spatulas and tongs made from heat-resistant materials created especially for use with nonstick cookware.

Sticky Butterscotch French Toast SERVES 4 TO 6

1 CUP (2 STICKS) UNSALTED BUTTER

1 CUP FIRMLY PACKED LIGHT BROWN SUGAR

1 CUP LYLE'S GOLDEN SYRUP, OR DARK CORN SYRUP

3 EGGS

1 CUP HEAVY CREAM

½ TEASPOON PURE VANILLA EXTRACT

¼ TEASPOON GROUND CINNAMON

SIX 1-INCH-THICK SLICES STALE OR DAY-OLD BRIOCHE, HAWAIIAN SWEET BREAD, OR OTHER SOFT EGG BREAD

IN A LARGE SAUCEPAN OVER MEDIUM HEAT, combine the butter, brown sugar, and golden syrup. Stir continuously until the butter and sugar melt together and combine with the syrup, 3 to 5 minutes. Increase the heat to medium-high and continue to simmer the syrup, bubbling gently, until thickened to the consistency of warm maple syrup, about 5 minutes. Remove from the heat and set aside.

IN A MEDIUM BOWL, whisk together the eggs, cream, vanilla, and cinnamon until smooth and combined.

SOAK EACH SLICE OF BREAD IN THE EGG AND CREAM MIXTURE, about 1 minute per side.

LIGHTLY COAT AN 8-INCH NONSTICK SKILLET WITH NONSTICK COOKING SPRAY. Place it over medium-high heat and add 2 to 3 tablespoons of the reserved syrup to create a light film over the bottom of the pan. When the syrup is hot and starts to bubble, add one slice of the soaked bread to the pan. Cook until the bread begins to absorb the syrup and sizzle and turn brown, 1 to 2 minutes. Flip the bread and cook until it is golden brown on both sides and cooked through, 1 to 2 minutes longer. Repeat this process with the remaining bread and syrup, wiping out the pan occasionally, if needed, to prevent burning.

SERVE THE FRENCH TOAST IMMEDIATELY, drizzled with the remaining warm butterscotch syrup, if desired, and with plenty of hot, crisp bacon on the side.

My great-grandmother and great-grandfather used to have a saying: "Eat like a king at breakfast, a prince at lunch, and a pauper at dinner." As a child, all I knew was they tucked into big slices of coconut cake, apple pie, or berry cobbler for breakfast. They were hard-working people, and burned off every calorie they ate taking care of their massive garden, canning fruits and vegetables in the heat of the summer, and chopping wood to stoke the fire for the wood-burning stove in their kitchen where they cooked all their meals. On the mornings when *you* wake up feeling particularly royal, give this apple pie–inspired stuffed French toast a whirl—you won't be disappointed.

A Is For Apple Pie–Stuffed French Toast SERVES 4

8 SLICES SLIGHTLY STALE BUTTERMILK BREAD OR POTATO BREAD

APPLE PIE COMPOTE (PAGE 34), AT ROOM TEMPERATURE

2 CUPS CORN FLAKES CEREAL, CRUSHED INTO COARSE CRUMBS

4 EGGS

1 CUP HALF-AND-HALF

1 TEASPOON PURE VANILLA EXTRACT

1 TABLESPOON GRANULATED SUGAR

4 TABLESPOONS UNSALTED BUTTER

4 TABLESPOONS VEGETABLE OIL

CONFECTIONERS' SUGAR FOR SPRINKLING

LAY 4 SLICES OF THE BREAD ON A FLAT WORK SURFACE. Top each slice with at least ¼ cup of the Apple Pie Compote, spreading it evenly. Top with the remaining slices of bread to form 4 sandwiches.

PLACE THE CEREAL CRUMBS ON A FLAT DINNER PLATE. In a large bowl, beat together the eggs, half-and-half, vanilla, and sugar until very smooth. Dip each sandwich into the egg mixture, turning it over to make sure it is well-soaked and completely coated. Dredge both sides of each sandwich completely in the cereal crumbs. Heat 2 tablespoons of the butter and 2 tablespoons of the oil in a large 10- or 12-inch nonstick skillet or frying pan, until the butter melts and starts to sizzle. Cook, 2 sandwiches at a time, until they are slightly puffed and crisp and golden brown all over, 2 to 3 minutes per side. Carefully wipe out the pan with a paper towel, and heat together the remaining 2 tablespoons butter and 2 tablespoons oil. Cook the remaining 2 sandwiches until crisp and golden brown.

REMOVE THE SANDWICHES FROM THE PAN AND PLACE ON A CUTTING BOARD. Cut each sandwich in half on the diagonal to expose the apple filling. Stack two halves onto an individual serving plate and sprinkle liberally with confectioners' sugar. Repeat with the remaining sandwiches and serve immediately.

Apple Primer

With so many apple varieties to choose from, it can be hard to pick just the right one for your applesauce, apple pie, or baked apple recipe.

Braeburn: This native New Zealander is crisp and aromatic with a good balance of tartness and sweetness. It is very juicy and makes a lovely applesauce.

Golden Delicious: This bright yellow apple is tender and juicy and makes good eating, is great in pies and tarts, and holds its shape without disintegrating or drying out.

Granny Smith: The Grand Dame of green apples, this all-purpose, sturdy beauty was the first green apple introduced to the American market. Its crisp, tangy flesh is tasty raw, but it truly comes into its own when cooked. Granny Smith apples are delicious sautéed in butter or baked in pies, and are a piquant addition when combined with softer, sweeter apples in applesauce.

Jonagold: This apple, a cross between Jonathan and Golden Delicious, is firm-fleshed, crisp, and sweet. It is wonderful raw, and makes delicious applesauce.

Jonathan: This round, red apple, often striped with creamy yellow, is crisp, sweet, and very juicy. Jonathan apples are delicious combined with other apples in both pies and applesauce.

McIntosh: This crimson-cheeked beauty, streaked with green and yellow, is sweet and aromatic. Its soft flesh makes this apple the perfect choice for applesauce.

Pippin: Like the Granny Smith, this crisp green apple makes deliciously tart eating, and holds its shape and rich flavor when sautéed or baked in a pie.

Spartan: This cross between a McIntosh and a Pippin is tender and sweet, with a mild acidity when raw. It cooks to a smooth, flavorful applesauce.

Apple Pie Compote

MAKES ABOUT 3 CUPS

3 TABLESPOONS UNSALTED BUTTER

3 LARGE GRANNY SMITH APPLES, PEELED, CORED, AND VERY THINLY SLICED

3 LARGE GOLDEN DELICIOUS, PINK LADY, OR MCINTOSH APPLES, PEELED, CORED, AND VERY THINLY SLICED

2½ CUPS GRANULATED SUGAR

¼ TEASPOON GROUND CINNAMON

⅛ TEASPOON FRESHLY GRATED NUTMEG

MELT THE BUTTER IN A LARGE SAUCEPAN OVER MEDIUM-LOW HEAT. Add the apples and sugar, cover, and cook, stirring occasionally, until the apples are tender and just starting to fall apart, about 30 minutes. Stir in the spices and continue cooking, uncovered, until the apples become completely soft, like a thick, glistening applesauce with tender chunks of apple strewn throughout.

NOTE: Don't blanch at the amount of sugar in this recipe. It really is more an apple jam than an applesauce, and would feel right at home spread on buttered toast or tucked into puff pastry squares for apple turnovers. You can even swirl it into rich Greek yogurt for a speedy breakfast. Make a big batch, and what you are not using in the French toast can be refrigerated for up to 1 week, or stored in covered containers in the freezer for up to 1 month.

What donut team do you root for? Yeast-raised donuts have their fans with their delicate melt-in-your-mouth quality, but I am definitely a cake donut girl myself. Often called "old-fashioned" donuts, cake donuts are very easy to make, and require about the same amount of time and skill to prepare as homemade biscuits. So put on your "Team Cake" T-shirt and whip up a batch of these fat, autumnal beauties. Their hearty, moist, and richly spiced flavor tastes like the first day of school, Halloween, and Thanksgiving all rolled into one.

Down-Home Praline and Pumpkin Spice Donuts

MAKES ABOUT 2 DOZEN DONUTS

4 CUPS ALL-PURPOSE FLOUR

2 TEASPOONS BAKING POWDER

1 TEASPOON BAKING SODA

1 TEASPOON GROUND CINNAMON

1 TEASPOON SALT

¼ TEASPOON FRESHLY GRATED NUTMEG

1 CUP FIRMLY PACKED DARK BROWN SUGAR

2 LARGE EGGS

¾ CUP SOUR CREAM

1 CUP CANNED PURE PUMPKIN PURÉE

1 TEASPOON PURE VANILLA EXTRACT

CANOLA OIL OR PEANUT OIL FOR FRYING

PRALINE ICING (PAGE 37) OR CINNAMON SUGAR (PAGE 37) FOR DREDGING

1 CUP CANDY SPRINKLES OR FINELY CHOPPED PECANS, TOASTED AND COOLED (OPTIONAL)

IN A LARGE BOWL, sift together the flour, baking powder, baking soda, cinnamon, salt, and nutmeg. In a separate bowl, whisk together the brown sugar, eggs, sour cream, pumpkin, and vanilla.

MAKE A WELL IN THE CENTER OF THE FLOUR MIXTURE AND POUR IN THE LIQUID INGREDIENTS. Using a wooden spoon, gradually stir the dry ingredients into the wet ingredients, just until a soft dough forms. The dough will be slightly sticky.

POUR THE DOUGH OUT ONTO A WELL-FLOURED WORK SURFACE. With lightly floured hands, carefully knead the dough, folding it over onto itself one or two times. Pat the dough out into a ½-inch-thick circle or rectangle. Cut out donuts using a 2 ½- to 3-inch donut cutter (alternatively use a biscuit cutter and a ¾-inch round cutter to cut a circle from the center.) Set aside the cut donuts. Reroll the scraps and cut out additional donuts. Use a pastry brush to remove excess flour from the donuts.

HEAT 4 INCHES OF OIL IN A LARGE DUTCH OVEN OR STOCKPOT OVER MEDIUM HIGH HEAT until it reaches 365°F to 375°F. (If you are using a deep-fat fryer or electric frying pan that can self-regulate the temperature of the oil, heat it to 350°F.) On the countertop next to your frying station, have ready bowls of warm Praline Icing and chopped pecans (if using) or Cinnamon Sugar. Set a wire rack over a paper towel–lined rimmed baking sheet.

FRY THE DONUTS, 3 or 4 at a time, turning once, until golden brown and cooked through, 2 to 3 minutes per side. Drain donuts briefly on the wire rack. When the donuts are cool enough to handle, but still warm, dip them in the Praline Icing and candy sprinkles or chopped pecans (if desired), or roll in the Cinnamon Sugar to coat well.

Straighten Up and Fry Right

You don't need a deep-fat fryer to make donuts, but having one makes the process particularly simple, as you can preset the temperature of the oil, and the fryer does the job of regulating it and keeping it steady. If using an electric frying pan or deep-fat fryer, set the temperature to 350°F. The fryer is able to regulate the temperature of the oil automatically and the donuts will cook through without burning.

If you are frying your donuts on top of the stove, use a large, heavy-bottomed stockpot or Dutch oven. You will need a candy/deep frying thermometer.

These thermometers are specifically designed to test the temperature of hot sugar syrups for homemade candy or hot oil for deep-fat frying. They are simple to use and attach to the side of the pot. Heat the oil to 375°F. After you add the donuts, the temperature will immediately drop to about 350°F. Keeping track of the temperature of the oil is very important, so make sure to use the thermometer. If the oil is too cool, the donuts will be leaden and greasy; if it is too hot, they will burn before they are cooked through. Candy/deep-frying thermometers are inexpensive and easy to find, and are available in most kitchenware and large department stores. They are well worth the small investment.

Praline Icing

MAKES ABOUT 2 CUPS

½ CUP (1 STICK) UNSALTED BUTTER, AT ROOM TEMPERATURE

1 CUP FIRMLY PACKED LIGHT BROWN SUGAR

¼ TEASPOON SALT

2 TABLESPOONS LIGHT CORN SYRUP

¼ CUP HEAVY CREAM

1 TEASPOON PURE VANILLA EXTRACT

1 TO 1½ CUPS CONFECTIONERS' SUGAR, SIFTED

IN A LARGE SAUCEPAN OVER MEDIUM HEAT, combine the butter, brown sugar, salt, and corn syrup. Cook, stirring to combine, until the butter melts and the sugar dissolves. Add the cream, increase the heat to high, and bring the mixture to a boil, stirring constantly. When the mixture boils, immediately remove from the heat and stir in the vanilla. Using a wooden spoon, beat in 1 cup of the confectioners' sugar. If the icing seems too thin, beat in the remaining ½ cup confectioners' sugar to thicken. If the icing starts to stiffen up too much as it cools, gently reheat over low heat to soften it, or stir in warm water, 1 tablespoon at a time, until it returns to the right consistency for dipping.

Cinnamon Sugar

MAKES 1 CUP

1 CUP GRANULATED SUGAR

1 TO 2 TEASPOONS GROUND CINNAMON

MIX THE SUGAR AND CINNAMON TOGETHER UNTIL WELL COMBINED.

Monkey bread is a fun recipe to make with children. Although there are recipes for monkey bread that use canned biscuit dough or frozen bread dough, I like to use this homemade tender and buttery sweet dough. If you are one of those bakers who turns the page as soon as you see the word "yeast," don't be afraid! This monkey bread is prepared in stages, so there are no worries about short attention spans or frayed nerves. Unlike making cakes or cookies that can come out tough and dry with rough handling, baking bread with children is a hoot—they can beat and pummel the dough to their hearts' content as they knead it. This dough is fairly simple, and it rises for the first time overnight in the refrigerator. The next day, have everyone pitch in and help roll the dough into little balls, dip them in melted butter, and then dip them in a thick coating of cinnamon-spiked brown sugar. The little balls of dough are tucked into a buttered-and-sugared Bundt pan and then allowed to rest in a warm place to rise a second time. Freshly baked, all warm and sticky, the plush, sugary pillows of bread are easy for small fingers—and big ones alike—to pull off and gobble up.

Curiously Sticky Caramel Monkey Bread

MAKES 1 LARGE MONKEY BREAD

SWEET DOUGH

1 CUP WARM (100°F TO 105°F) WHOLE MILK

½ CUP GRANULATED SUGAR

1 PACKAGE (¼ OUNCE) ACTIVE DRY YEAST

5 CUPS UNBLEACHED ALL-PURPOSE FLOUR

½ CUP (1 STICK) UNSALTED BUTTER, AT ROOM TEMPERATURE

2 LARGE EGGS

1¼ TEASPOONS SALT

ROLLING MIXTURE

1 CUP (2 STICKS) UNSALTED BUTTER, MELTED

2½ CUPS FIRMLY PACKED DARK BROWN SUGAR

2 TEASPOONS GROUND CINNAMON

TO MAKE THE DOUGH: One day before serving the bread, pour the warm milk into a large bowl of a stand mixer. Stir in the sugar and sprinkle the yeast over the surface of the milk. Let the mixture stand until the yeast thickens and starts to bubble, about 5 minutes. Using the paddle attachment, mix in 2 cups of the flour, the softened butter, and the eggs, at low speed. Add the salt and enough of the remaining flour to form a soft dough.

SCRAPE THE DOUGH OUT ONTO A LIGHTLY FLOURED SURFACE AND KNEAD BY HAND, using the heel of your hand to push the dough away from you and then pulling it back over on itself. Repeat this process until the dough is smooth and elastic, 8 to 10 minutes. Alternatively, knead the dough in the electric mixer using the dough hook for 8 to 10 minutes. The dough should be silky, with a subtle sheen, and when shaped into a round loaf, as smooth and firm as a baby's bottom.

BUTTER A LARGE BOWL AND ADD THE DOUGH, turning to coat all sides with the butter. Cover the bowl loosely with plastic wrap and refrigerate overnight to rise slowly.

THE NEXT DAY, PREPARE THE ROLLING MIXTURE: Place the melted butter in a small bowl. In a separate dish, stir together the brown sugar and cinnamon. Remove the dough from the refrigerator and punch down. Cut the dough, using a sharp knife, into four equal portions. Pinch each section of dough into approximately 1-ounce portions and roll into small balls. You should have about 40 balls of dough.

The Big Sleep

Why is the dough refrigerated overnight? Besides making the process of preparing the monkey bread much easier by breaking the steps up over 2 days, a slow, cold rise in the refrigerator allows the yeast to work slowly, so the rich flavors of this sweet dough have time to fully develop. The final bread will have a rounder, more complex, and therefore exceptional flavor.

"The best thing about baking is licking your hands."
Taylor Seay, age 7

COAT A NONSTICK BUNDT PAN VERY LIGHTLY WITH NONSTICK COOKING SPRAY AND BRUSH liberally with 3 tablespoons of the melted butter. Sprinkle the buttered Bundt pan evenly with ½ cup of the brown sugar–cinnamon mixture. Roll each ball of dough in the remaining melted butter and then roll liberally in the remaining brown sugar–cinnamon mixture. Layer the balls lightly in the pan. The pan will hold 35 to 37 balls of dough (save any remaining balls to bake separately in a small pan to give to your helpers as "testers"). Leave a 1-inch to 1½-inch space between the balls and the rim of the Bundt pan to allow the dough room to rise. Drizzle any remaining melted butter over the dough, cover loosely with plastic wrap, and let rise again for 45 to 60 minutes in a warm place.

WHILE THE DOUGH IS RISING, set a rack in the middle of the oven and preheat the oven to 350°F.

BAKE THE MONKEY BREAD UNTIL THE BREAD IS PUFFED AND GOLDEN AND COOKED THROUGH, 30 to 35 minutes. Let cool on a wire rack for about 5 minutes before inverting onto a serving platter. Let cool for another 3 to 5 minutes before removing the pan. Serve while still warm.

2

Every Day's a Holiday

Simple Treats that Make
Every Day Special

When I was growing up there was often a homemade treat waiting for my brothers and me when we came home from school:

Cold pitchers of lemonade to wash down big bowls of popcorn drizzled with melted butter; freshly baked cookies cooling or a simple snack cake sprinkled with confectioners' sugar; or homemade chocolate pudding chilling in a big Pyrex dish in our refrigerator (uncovered, because my mom's favorite part was the chewy skin that formed on the surface as it cooled).

Baking from scratch doesn't have to be difficult or time consuming. With a few pantry staples and basic kitchen equipment, you can make every day a special occasion for yourself, your children, and anyone lucky enough to visit your home. Sure, you can buy delicious treats from a bakery, but nothing will perfume your house like a quick batch of Chock-a-Block Chocolate Chip Gingerbread Muffins, or taste as good as a fresh fruit crumble pulled warm and bubbling from your oven. Everyone can stir together soft, deliciously chewy cookies to rival any bakery with my recipe for Hunka Chunka Chewy Chocolate Chip Cookies using equipment no more complicated than a bowl and a wooden spoon. For a fun weeknight dessert, make Houdini's Hot Chocolate Pudding Cake—part dessert, part science experiment. The batter goes into the oven covered with a mixture of cocoa and boiling water only to emerge as a moist, gooey, chocolate cake with its own built-in chocolate sauce—no bakery can rival that.

Do you remember Willy Wonka's Fizzy Lifting Drinks that made Charlie and his Grandpa Joe float to the ceiling after they drank too much? Here is my version and I think it beats soda any day. It's fresh, tangy, and a sparkling blush pink. I love serving this at parties because it suits both children and adults, and you can make the berry purée and the flavor base of sweetened citrus juice well ahead of time, stirring in the sparkling water just before you are ready to serve. You can substitute fresh lime juice for the lemon, and stir in blackberry purée for a wonderful fizzy drink the color of lavender. If you can find it, use superfine granulated sugar sometimes called "baker's sugar" or "bar sugar." It dissolves easily and leaves no grittiness in the drink.

Fizzy Lemonade Sparklers

MAKES 1 GALLON

1½ TO 2 CUPS SUPERFINE SUGAR

2 CUPS FRESH LEMON JUICE (OR SUBSTITUTE FRESH LIME JUICE)

1 GALLON SPARKLING WATER OR CLUB SODA

1 CUP STRAWBERRY PURÉE (RECIPE FOLLOWS), OR SUBSTITUTE RASPBERRY OR BLACKBERRY PURÉE (PAGE 45)

IN A LARGE PITCHER, stir together the sugar and lemon juice until the sugar is dissolved. Refrigerate until ready to serve.

RIGHT BEFORE SERVING, stir the sparkling water and fruit purée into the sweetened lemon juice. Serve immediately.

Strawberry Purée

MAKES 2 TO 2½ CUPS

1 POUND FROZEN STRAWBERRIES (UNSWEETENED)

2 TABLESPOONS GRANULATED SUGAR

THAW STRAWBERRIES COMPLETELY, reserving any accumulated juices. Purée the fruit and juices in a food processor or blender until smooth. Stir in the sugar and taste for sweetness. Add more sugar if desired. Refrigerate purée in a covered container for up to 1 week.

Sugar, Refined

If you can't find superfine sugar, it's easy to make your own: Pulse regular granulated sugar in a food processor fitted with the stainless-steel chopping blade, using on-off motions, until the sugar is fine and powdery, 30 to 60 seconds.

Raspberry Purée

MAKES 1½ TO 2 CUPS

1 POUND FROZEN RASPBERRIES
(UNSWEETENED)

2 TABLESPOONS GRANULATED SUGAR

THAW RASPBERRIES COMPLETELY, reserving any accumulated juices. Purée the fruit and juices in a food processor or blender until smooth. Using the back of a large spoon, press the purée through a fine-meshed sieve into a bowl. Discard the remaining seeds. Stir in the sugar and taste for sweetness. Add more sugar if desired. Refrigerate purée in a covered container for up to 1 week.

Blackberry Purée

MAKES 1½ TO 2 CUPS

1 POUND FROZEN BLACKBERRIES
(UNSWEETENED)

2 TABLESPOONS GRANULATED SUGAR

THAW BLACKBERRIES COMPLETELY, reserving any accumulated juices. Purée the fruit and juices in a food processor or blender until smooth. Using the back of a large spoon, press the purée through a fine-meshed sieve into a bowl. Discard the remaining seeds. Stir in the sugar and taste for sweetness. Add more sugar if desired. Refrigerate purée in a covered container for up to 1 week.

There is nothing like watching a group of 7-year-olds taste a batch of chocolate chip cookies—they do so with the same intensity and concentration usually reserved for sampling a fine, aged Bordeaux. These big, fat, saucer-size cookies are crisp around the edges but lusciously soft and chewy in the center. Chock-full of chips and picture perfect, they have been sampled many times to great acclaim— touted as much for their simplicity as their flavor. Starting the batter with melted butter keeps these cookies chewy and dense, and chilling the dough for a little while before baking yields cookies that one young tester told me "look like they came from the bakery." Compliments, indeed.

Hunka Chunka Chewy Chocolate Chip Cookies

MAKES 18 BIG COOKIES

1 CUP (2 STICKS) UNSALTED BUTTER, MELTED AND COOLED

1 CUP FIRMLY PACKED DARK BROWN SUGAR

1 CUP GRANULATED SUGAR

1 TABLESPOON PURE VANILLA EXTRACT

2 EGGS, PLUS 1 EGG YOLK

3 CUPS ALL-PURPOSE FLOUR

1 TEASPOON BAKING SODA

1 TEASPOON SALT

3 CUPS SEMISWEET CHOCOLATE CHIPS

LINE 2 BAKING SHEETS WITH PARCHMENT PAPER OR COAT LIGHTLY WITH NONSTICK COOKING spray. Set aside.

IN A LARGE BOWL, mix together the melted butter, sugars, vanilla, eggs, and egg yolk. Sift the flour, baking soda, and salt into the bowl and stir the ingredients together to form a soft dough. Stir in the chocolate chips.

USING A 2-OUNCE SELF-RELEASING ICE-CREAM SCOOP OR A ¼-CUP MEASURING CUP, form large balls of cookie dough. Place on a parchment paper–lined baking sheet, 9 to a sheet to allow room for spreading, and chill the dough for at least 30 minutes or up to overnight.

PREHEAT THE OVEN TO 350°F.

BAKE THE COOKIES UNTIL THEY ARE GOLDEN BROWN AND CRISP AROUND THE EDGES BUT still slightly soft in the center, 15 to 17 minutes. Transfer to a wire rack and allow cookies to cool completely on the baking sheet before eating.

"Mommy, why can't you make cookies like the store?"
Abigail Lightfoot, age 4, to her mother after sampling her aunt's first batch of
Hunka Chunka Chewy Chocolate Chip Cookies

Sunflower seed butter has proven itself a new food superhero for many people, mainly children who suffer from peanut allergies. Sun butter and jelly sandwiches are becoming a new standard in school cafeterias that have been deemed "peanut-free zones." Sun butter's earthy flavor and creamy texture make it a wonderful substitute for peanut butter in these cookie jar favorites traditionally topped with a creamy milk chocolate kiss. Or you can prepare them like classic peanut butter cookies, rolled in a shiny jacket of sugar and crosshatched with a fork before baking.

Sun Butter Blossoms

MAKES 3½ TO 4 DOZEN COOKIES

¾ CUP (1½ STICKS) UNSALTED BUTTER, AT ROOM TEMPERATURE

¾ CUP SUN BUTTER

1 CUP FIRMLY PACKED DARK BROWN SUGAR

⅓ CUP GRANULATED SUGAR

2 EGGS

1 TEASPOON FRESH LEMON JUICE

2 TABLESPOONS MOLASSES

2 TEASPOONS PURE VANILLA EXTRACT

2 CUPS ALL-PURPOSE FLOUR

¾ TEASPOON BAKING SODA

½ TEASPOON SALT

GRANULATED SUGAR, DEMERARA SUGAR, OR RAW SUGAR FOR ROLLING

42 TO 48 MILK CHOCOLATE KISSES, UNWRAPPED

IN A LARGE BOWL, beat together the butter, sun butter, brown sugar, and granulated sugar until creamy. Beat in the eggs, lemon juice, molasses, and vanilla. Sift together the flour, baking soda, and salt and stir into the batter just until combined.

COVER AND REFRIGERATE THE DOUGH JUST UNTIL FIRM ENOUGH TO ROLL INTO BALLS, no more than 2 hours. (The dough does not need to be completely firm to roll into balls; if it is still soft when you are ready to bake the cookies, use a miniature ice-cream scoop to portion out the dough, drop in the granulated sugar, and roll lightly before placing on the baking sheet.)

PREHEAT THE OVEN TO 375°F. Line 2 baking sheets with parchment paper, or coat with nonstick cooking spray. Roll the dough into 1-inch balls and then roll the balls liberally in granulated, demerara, or raw sugar. Place the balls on the prepared baking sheets, at least 2 inches apart to allow for spreading. Bake until slightly puffed and turning golden brown, 8 to 10 minutes. Remove the cookies from the oven and immediately press a chocolate kiss into the center of each cookie while they are still warm. Let cool for 5 minutes on the cookie sheet before removing and cooling completely on a wire rack.

ALTERNATIVELY, eliminate the chocolate kiss, and, after rolling the dough in sugar, press crosshatch marks into the cookies with a fork before baking.

Hey, Mr. Science!

My Sun Butter Blossoms turned green! Sunflower seed butter is rich in chlorogenic acid, which, in an alkaline-rich batter, can oxidize and turn green. Baking soda, which is added to many cookie recipes, is a powerful alkaline that helps cookies rise and bake to a rich golden brown, gives them a chewy texture, and—in this case—may turn the cookie green! Green sun butter cookies are harmless, but to avoid this phenomenon, it's best not to refrigerate the dough for too long before making the cookies; bake them as soon as the dough is firm enough to roll into balls. Also, keep the batter *acidic* by using more brown sugar than white, and adding a little molasses and lemon juice. I also reduced the amount of baking soda from 1 teaspoon to ¾ teaspoon, which will still get the job done, but should prevent these cookies from doing their best imitation of "The Incredible Hulk."

"Earthy . . . but I like it."
Olivia O'Connor, 15, cookie connoisseur

My well-thumbed copies of *Home Cooking* and *More Home Cooking*, collections of wonderful food essays by the late Laurie Colwin, have transported me many times into this author's charmed vision of domestic and culinary bliss. I love reading and rereading about her idiosyncratic food loves—the perfect Thanksgiving stuffing, her passion for a well-cooked Brussels sprout, and the comfort found in a mug of homemade beef tea. Gingerbread, with its peppery sweet flavor and pungent aroma, was one of her favorites, and it was Colwin who first planted the idea in my head to combine ginger with chocolate. Her favorite birthday cake combined dark, sticky layers of gingerbread sandwiched with raspberry jam and iced thickly with chocolate frosting. In honor of Ms. Colwin and her love of all things dark and spicy, I created these easy-to-make gingerbread muffins speckled with chocolate chips—their spicy scent ready to perfume your house and feed anyone who may be hungry at three o'clock in the afternoon.

Chock-a-Block Chocolate Chip Gingerbread Muffins MAKES 18 MUFFINS

2¼ CUPS PLUS 1 TABLESPOON ALL-PURPOSE FLOUR

1 TEASPOON BAKING SODA

1 TEASPOON BAKING POWDER

½ TEASPOON SALT

2 TEASPOONS GROUND CINNAMON

1 TABLESPOON GROUND GINGER

½ TEASPOON GROUND NUTMEG

½ CUP (1 STICK) UNSALTED BUTTER

1½ CUPS FIRMLY PACKED DARK BROWN SUGAR

1 CUP MOLASSES

1 CUP BUTTERMILK

2 LARGE EGGS

½ CUP BREWED COFFEE

1½ TO 2 CUPS MINIATURE SEMISWEET CHOCOLATE CHIPS

CONFECTIONERS' SUGAR FOR SPRINKLING

PREHEAT THE OVEN TO 350°F. Line 18 standard-size muffin cups with paper liners.

IN A LARGE BOWL, sift together the 2¼ cups flour, the baking soda, baking powder, salt, cinnamon, ginger, and nutmeg. Set aside.

IN A MEDIUM SAUCEPAN OVER MEDIUM HEAT, combine the butter, brown sugar, and molasses. Stir together just until the butter melts and the sugar dissolves forming a thick syrup. Do not boil. Remove from the heat and stir in the buttermilk, eggs, and coffee. Gradually whisk the wet ingredients into the dry ingredients, whisking only until combined. Let the batter cool completely. Toss the chocolate chips with the remaining 1 tablespoon flour and fold into the batter. (Make sure the batter is cool before stirring in the chocolate chips; if the batter is too hot, the chocolate chips will melt.)

FILL THE MUFFIN CUPS THREE-FOURTHS FULL OF BATTER, and bake until a skewer inserted into the center comes out clean, 18 to 22 minutes. Let cool completely. Sprinkle with confectioners' sugar.

WANT SOMETHING A LITTLE FANCIER? Leave out the chocolate chips (or not!) and frost the cooled gingerbread muffins with a little Cream Cheese Icing (page 52) instead. Delish.

Slower than...

Dark, rich molasses is what gives gingerbread its distinctive, sweet, and slightly smoky flavor. A by-product in the manufacture of white sugar, molasses is a thick, robust syrup produced when the sugar is being separated from the juice of the sugarcane. Along with a distinctive flavor and a deep, rich color, molasses adds moisture and tenderness to cookies and cakes.

Baking Know-How

Why do I have to beat the sugar and butter together?
When you beat butter and sugar together until it is light and fluffy, this is called *creaming*. When you cream together butter and sugar to make a cake, you are beating air into the mixture. This helps your cake rise and become light and delicate in texture.

Why do the bananas have to be so ripe?
The riper the banana, the softer and sweeter it will be. It will also have the strongest banana flavor. Soft, ripe, banana purée is easier to mix into the other ingredients and makes a sweeter, moister cake.

Cream Cheese Icing

MAKES ABOUT 2½ CUPS

8 OUNCES CREAM CHEESE, AT ROOM TEMPERATURE

4 TABLESPOONS UNSALTED BUTTER, AT ROOM TEMPERATURE

1 POUND CONFECTIONERS' SUGAR, SIFTED

1 TEASPOON PURE VANILLA EXTRACT

PINCH OF SALT

COMBINE THE CREAM CHEESE AND BUTTER IN A MEDIUM BOWL. Using an electric mixer set at medium speed, beat together. Add the confectioners' sugar, vanilla, and salt, beating until creamy.

The sad fact is that gingerbread is on the decline, although it is alive and well in children's books of the fifties, where cheerful housewives wait at home for the arrival of their hungry children at three o'clock, ready with a great pan of warm gingerbread and some ice cold milk.
from More Home Cooking, *by Laurie Colwin*

On cold rainy days, when everyone arrives home from school and work cranky and wet, the aroma of something warm and sweet coming from the oven can do wonders for the mood. It's always good to have a bunch of bananas on your counter, ripening and ready to make a delicious little cake like this one. The riper the bananas, the sweeter and more flavorful your batter will be. They should be very soft, needing no more than the gentle pressure of a fork to coax them into a thick purée. Be sure to use cake flour—it gives this cake an extra-velvety texture.

Banana Montana After-School Cake

SERVES 9

1¾ CUPS CAKE FLOUR

1 TEASPOON BAKING POWDER

¾ TEASPOON BAKING SODA

½ TEASPOON SALT

½ CUP (1 STICK) UNSALTED BUTTER, AT ROOM TEMPERATURE

½ CUP GRANULATED SUGAR

½ CUP FIRMLY PACKED LIGHT BROWN SUGAR

2 EGGS, AT ROOM TEMPERATURE

1 TEASPOON PURE VANILLA EXTRACT

1 CUP MASHED VERY RIPE BANANA

¼ CUP BUTTERMILK

¾ CUP DICED PECANS, TOASTED AND COOLED (OPTIONAL)

CONFECTIONERS' SUGAR FOR SPRINKLING

PREHEAT THE OVEN TO 350°F. Coat the bottom and sides of an 8-inch or 9-inch square cake pan with nonstick cooking spray.

IN A MEDIUM BOWL, sift together the flour, baking powder, baking soda, and salt. Set aside.

IN A SEPARATE BOWL, combine the butter, granulated sugar, and brown sugar. Using an electric mixer set at medium speed, beat together until light and fluffy, 3 to 4 minutes. Beat in the eggs, one at a time, and then beat in the vanilla, bananas, and buttermilk, just until combined.

WITH THE MIXER SET AT LOW SPEED, beat the flour mixture into the banana batter, in two additions, just until combined. Do not overbeat the batter. Using a rubber spatula, stir the pecans (if using) into the batter.

SPREAD THE BATTER INTO THE PREPARED PAN IN AN EVEN LAYER AND BAKE UNTIL FIRM AND golden brown and a skewer inserted into the center of the cake comes out clean, about 50 minutes.

TRANSFER TO A WIRE RACK AND LET COOL FOR 15 MINUTES. Sprinkle with confectioners' sugar and cut into 9 squares. Serve warm.

Angel biscuits are a great introduction to working with yeast. Sometimes referred to as "Bride's Biscuits," they are nearly foolproof because the yeast dough is propped up by two additional leavening agents—baking powder and baking soda—making them the ultimate homemade dinner roll for nervous first-time bakers. Part tender dinner roll and part flaky biscuit, they are as fabulous to eat as they are easy to make. When pulled open, all moist and steaming, their creamy bellies make the perfect resting spot for pools of melted butter, homemade jam, or a golden drizzle of honey. I think they are the ideal biscuit for Thanksgiving dinner, as their flavor benefits from a slow and sleepy rise in the refrigerator overnight. Just remove the dough from the refrigerator, shape, and let the biscuits rise in a warm spot for about 30 minutes. Bake them after you pull the turkey from the oven and you will have warm, moist biscuits ready to smother in butter or dip in the gravy by the time the turkey is carved and ready to serve.

Heaven-Sent Angel Biscuits

MAKES ABOUT 2 DOZEN BISCUITS

1 PACKAGE (1 TABLESPOON) ACTIVE DRY YEAST

½ CUP WARM WATER

5½ CUPS UNBLEACHED ALL-PURPOSE FLOUR

1 TEASPOON BAKING SODA

1 TABLESPOON BAKING POWDER

1 TEASPOON SALT

¼ CUP GRANULATED SUGAR

12 TABLESPOONS VERY COLD VEGETABLE SHORTENING, CUT INTO 12 PIECES

4 TABLESPOONS VERY COLD UNSALTED BUTTER

2 CUPS COLD BUTTERMILK

IN A SMALL BOWL, sprinkle the yeast over the warm water and set aside.

IN A LARGE BOWL, sift together the flour, baking soda, baking powder, salt, and sugar.

USING A PASTRY BLENDER OR YOUR HANDS, rub the cold shortening and butter into the flour mixture until it resembles coarse breadcrumbs with a few large pea-size bits of butter strewn throughout the mixture.

MAKE A WELL IN THE CENTER OF THE FLOUR AND POUR IN THE BUTTERMILK AND THE YEAST mixture. Combine the dry ingredients into the wet ingredients using one hand, stirring in a circular motion to draw more flour into the liquid until it forms a soft dough.

PAT THE DOUGH INTO A LARGE LOAF, and store in a 2-gallon self-sealing plastic bag. Refrigerate overnight.

THE NEXT DAY, pinch off portions of the dough and form into ping-pong ball–size rolls. Place the rolls on a buttered baking sheet, about ¼ inch apart. Cover lightly with plastic wrap and let rise in a warm place for about 30 minutes before baking.

WHILE THE BISCUITS ARE RISING, preheat the oven to 425°F.

BAKE THE BISCUITS UNTIL RISEN AND GOLDEN BROWN ON TOP, 12 to 15 minutes. Serve warm.

As a college student, I spent a semester in London soaking up as much beer and culture as I possibly could. Low on funds, I subsisted mostly on take-away doner kebabs, McVitie's chocolate biscuits, and strong tea. When I was able to cobble together enough money to venture into a restaurant, I went with friends to a little café called Oodles. The food was plain but plentiful, and I always ended my meal with a sweet and chewy oatmeal flapjack, which they cut into large slabs and displayed haphazardly on tiered cake stands by the till. At the time, I didn't realize how very easy flapjacks were to make at home; they are a simple mixture of oats, melted butter, brown sugar, and a sticky dollop of Lyle's Golden Syrup—a natural cane sugar syrup much loved by British bakers for its buttery, caramel-like flavor. Lyle's Golden Syrup is available in the United States, or you can use honey instead.

Ode to Oodles Oatmeal Flapjacks MAKES 10 BARS

¾ CUP (1½ STICKS) UNSALTED BUTTER

½ CUP LYLE'S GOLDEN SYRUP OR HONEY

1 CUP FIRMLY PACKED DARK BROWN SUGAR

1 TEASPOON PURE VANILLA EXTRACT

½ TEASPOON SALT

3 CUPS OLD-FASHIONED ROLLED OATS

2 CUPS SEMISWEET CHOCOLATE CHIPS (OPTIONAL)

"You know what goes with brown sugar? Brown sugar."
Sophia O'Connor, age 7, sugar aficionada

PREHEAT THE OVEN TO 350°F. Line an 8-inch or 9-inch square pan with parchment paper or nonstick foil and coat lightly with nonstick spray.

IN A LARGE STOCKPOT OR DUTCH OVEN OVER MEDIUM HEAT, combine the butter, golden syrup, and brown sugar. Stir until the butter and sugar melt together. Bring to a boil and cook for about 10 seconds. Remove from the heat and stir in the vanilla and salt. Stir in the oats until they are completely covered in the syrup.

SPOON THE OAT MIXTURE INTO THE PREPARED PAN AND PRESS VERY FIRMLY INTO THE PAN. Bake until very golden brown and crisp around the edges, about 30 minutes. Remove from the oven and let cool completely on a wire rack. Turn out onto a cutting board and peel away the parchment or foil. Using a sharp knife, cut into 5 long strips and cut each strip in half.

TO DECORATE THE COOKIE BARS WITH CHOCOLATE (IF USING): Spread the chocolate chips in a single layer on a large heatproof dinner plate. Place the plate, uncovered, in the microwave and heat on half-power for 1 minute. Check the chocolate; if it is soft and shiny, stir it until it is melted and smooth. If the chocolate is not soft enough to stir smooth, continue heating it in the microwave in 30-second intervals and stir until smooth. Scrape the chocolate into a small bowl and dip the ends of the flapjacks in the chocolate. Place the dipped bars on a parchment-lined baking sheet to let the chocolate harden. Alternatively, drizzle the melted chocolate over the bars with a fork. Eat immediately, or store in a tightly covered container for up to 3 days.

OPTIONS: Before baking, add 1 cup of any of the following to the oat mixture: mini chocolate chips, chopped nuts, raisins, dried cranberries, dried cherries, diced dried apricots, sweetened flaked coconut.

Do you nibble around the edges first? Do you swallow it quickly in two big bites? If you can tell me in vivid detail how you eat a Reese's Peanut Butter Cup, then this luscious pudding is especially for you. Made with half-and-half, a double dose of chocolate, and a dollop of creamy peanut butter, the flavor is intense and continues to blossom as it chills in the refrigerator. Rich and thick enough to stand your spoon in, these pudding cups are best eaten in small doses. For a softer texture, make the pudding with whole milk instead of half-and-half. Both methods produce a delicious result.

Wicked Good Chocolate Peanut Butter Pudding Cups

SERVES 8

¼ CUP CORNSTARCH

¾ CUP GRANULATED SUGAR

¼ TEASPOON SALT

¼ CUP DUTCH-PROCESSED COCOA POWDER

3½ CUPS HALF-AND-HALF OR WHOLE MILK

6 LARGE EGG YOLKS

1 TEASPOON PURE VANILLA EXTRACT

⅓ CUP CREAMY PEANUT BUTTER

½ CUP (HEAPED) SEMISWEET CHOCOLATE CHIPS

WHIPPED CREAM FOR TOPPING

CHOCOLATE JIMMIES FOR SPRINKLING

INTO A MEDIUM SAUCEPAN, sift together the cornstarch, sugar, salt, and cocoa powder. Slowly whisk in the half-and-half until the mixture is combined and smooth. Whisk in the egg yolks, one at a time, until smooth.

COOK THE PUDDING OVER MEDIUM HEAT, whisking continuously, until the pudding starts to thicken and large bubbles form and plop, like slowly bubbling hot lava, on the surface of the pudding. Reduce the heat to low, and continue cooking, stirring continuously for 1 minute. Check the consistency of the pudding by running your finger across the back of the stirring spoon; if it leaves a trail that does not immediately fill in, it is thick enough.

REMOVE FROM THE HEAT AND STIR THE VANILLA, peanut butter, and chocolate chips into the hot pudding until thoroughly melted and combined.

PLACE EIGHT 4-OUNCE CUSTARD CUPS OR RAMEKINS ON A RIMMED BAKING SHEET. Pour the pudding into the cups, using a damp paper towel to clean up any drips. Cover the custard cups with plastic wrap. Alternatively, pour the pudding into a large bowl and cover the surface of the pudding with plastic wrap to prevent a skin from forming. Refrigerate the pudding until very cold, at least 4 hours and up to overnight.

TO SERVE, top the custard cups with a dollop of whipped cream and a sprinkling of chocolate jimmies (also called chocolate vermicelli). If refrigerated in the larger bowl, you can scoop it into small dessert dishes or the Chocolate Balloon Cups (page 88) and top with whipped cream and chocolate jimmies.

Separating Eggs

1   To separate the egg yolk from the egg white, it is best to start with ice-cold eggs. If the eggs are too warm, the yolk is more likely to break apart into the white as you separate them.

2   Have two small bowls ready, and crack the egg, near the center, sharply against the side of one bowl.

3   Hold the egg over one bowl and pry the two halves of the shell apart with your fingers, carefully catching the yolk in one half of the shell, and letting the white drip into the bowl. You will still have some of the white clinging to the yolk.

4   Transfer the yolk back and forth from one shell half to the other, all the while allowing more and more of the white to drip into the bowl below.

5   Drop the yolk into the second bowl, and discard the egg shells.

Going Dutch (Cocoa, that is)

What is Dutch-processed cocoa? There are two kinds of cocoa powder: Dutch-processed and natural. Dusky brown, natural cocoa powder has a hearty flavor, but can be very acidic and bitter. It works best in recipes that are leavened with baking soda or in recipes that call for lots of sugar, like brownies. Dutch-processed cocoa powder, on the other hand, is processed with an alkali that tempers the natural acidity and bitterness of cocoa, giving it a milder, richer flavor that performs beautifully in a variety of chocolate-flavored desserts from sorbets and hot cocoas, to puddings, custards, and European-style cakes. Tempering the acidity in the cocoa also enhances the flavor and darkens the color of the cocoa, so desserts like the Wicked Good Chocolate Peanut Butter Pudding Cups look and taste darker and richer.

Even without tarot cards, a crystal ball, or a wizard's wand, this recipe is pure culinary magic. A simple chocolate cake batter is covered, alarmingly, in a boiling water and cocoa mixture before it is baked, and, voila! It transforms itself in the oven—the batter levitates, leaving a gooey puddinglike sauce beneath a moist, fudgy, layer of chocolate cake. Be careful not to rush it—let the cake rest for about 15 minutes after it comes out of the oven before you dig in to experience the true wonder of this warm, simple dessert. Oh, and your lovely assistant? Why, a scoop of vanilla ice cream, of course.

Houdini's Hot Chocolate Pudding Cake
SERVES 4 TO 6

1¼ CUPS WHOLE MILK

½ CUP (HEAPED) SEMISWEET CHOCOLATE CHIPS, OR 4 OUNCES SEMISWEET CHOCOLATE, FINELY CHOPPED

1 TEASPOON PURE VANILLA EXTRACT

½ CUP (1 STICK) UNSALTED BUTTER, AT ROOM TEMPERATURE

½ CUP GRANULATED SUGAR

¼ CUP DUTCH-PROCESSED COCOA POWDER

1⅓ CUPS ALL-PURPOSE FLOUR

1½ TEASPOONS BAKING POWDER

½ TEASPOON SALT

CHOCOLATE SAUCE

¼ CUP DUTCH-PROCESSED COCOA POWDER, SIFTED

1 CUP FIRMLY PACKED DARK BROWN SUGAR

1⅓ CUPS BOILING WATER

PREHEAT THE OVEN TO 350°F. Butter a 1-quart ceramic soufflé dish or an 8-inch square baking pan.

IN A SMALL SAUCEPAN OVER MEDIUM HEAT, combine the milk, chocolate, and vanilla. Stir just until the chocolate chips are melted and the mixture is smooth and combined. Do not boil. Remove from the heat and let cool slightly.

IN A MEDIUM BOWL, beat the butter and sugar together with a hand-held mixer set at medium speed until light and fluffy, 3 to 4 minutes. Slowly beat in the chocolate mixture until combined. Sift the cocoa powder, flour, baking powder, and salt into the butter mixture and beat just until smooth. Do not overbeat.

SPREAD THE BATTER EVENLY INTO THE PREPARED DISH.

TO MAKE THE CHOCOLATE SAUCE: In a small bowl stir together the cocoa powder, brown sugar, and boiling water until dissolved. Carefully spoon this mixture over the surface of the cake batter. The sauce may sink into the batter and begin to separate; don't worry. Be sure to spoon all the sauce over the cake and bake immediately in the preheated oven for 30 to 35 minutes. The cake will rise completely above the sauce and should be puffy and firm around the edges, but may still be slightly soft in the center. Transfer to a wire rack to let cool for about 15 minutes before serving. Cooling allows the cake to settle and the warm sauce to thicken slightly underneath. Scoop portions of the cake and sauce into individual dessert dishes and serve warm.

There is nothing easier or more cozily down-home to serve after dinner than a homemade fruit crumble warm from the oven. It isn't fussy or fancy, but this old-fashioned dessert will be welcome on any occasion. I love the sweet-tart combination of blackberries and apples. And the crumble—made with a healthful dose of oatmeal, a little whole wheat flour, and the crunch of raw sugar—makes for a buttery, sweetly nutty-tasting, crisp topping.

Quickberry! Quackberry! Blackberry-Apple Crumble

SERVES 6 TO 8

CRUMBLE TOPPING

½ CUP ALL-PURPOSE FLOUR

½ CUP WHOLE WHEAT FLOUR

1 CUP QUICK-COOKING (NOT OLD-FASHIONED ROLLED) OATS

1 CUP RAW SUGAR OR DEMERARA SUGAR

¼ TEASPOON SALT

¾ CUP (1½ STICKS) UNSALTED BUTTER, MELTED

FRUIT FILLING

4 LARGE GOLDEN DELICIOUS APPLES, PEELED, CORED, AND THINLY SLICED

2 TO 3 CUPS FRESH BLACKBERRIES

½ CUP GRANULATED SUGAR

2 TABLESPOONS CORNSTARCH

WHIPPED CREAM OR ICE CREAM FOR SERVING (OPTIONAL)

SET A RACK IN THE MIDDLE OF THE OVEN AND PREHEAT THE OVEN TO 350°F.

TO PREPARE THE CRUMBLE TOPPING: In a medium bowl, stir together the all-purpose and whole wheat flours, oats, sugar, and salt. Stir in the melted butter until the mixture is thoroughly moistened and resembles coarse bread crumbs. Set aside.

TO PREPARE THE FILLING: In a large bowl, toss together the fruit, sugar, and cornstarch. Spread the fruit evenly into a buttered 9-by-13-inch glass or ceramic baking dish.

SPREAD THE TOPPING EVENLY OVER THE FRUIT with your fingers, making sure the fruit is completely covered. Bake until the crumble topping is crisp and brown, the fruit is tender, and the juices are bubbling thickly around the topping, about 45 minutes. For individual servings, divide the fruit among six 6-ounce buttered ramekins or ceramic baking dishes. Top each dish with an equal amount of the crumble and place the ramekins on a baking sheet. Bake 35 to 45 minutes. Remove from the oven and transfer to a wire rack. Allow the crumble to cool slightly for at least 10 to 15 minutes before serving. Serve warm with whipped cream or vanilla ice cream, if desired.

Quickberry! Quackberry! Pick me a blackberry!
Trainberry, Trackberry, Clickety-clackberry
Rumble and ramble
In blackberry bramble
Billions of berries
For blackberry jamble.
from Jamberry, by Bruce Degen

3

Get This Party Started

Irresistible Desserts that
Take Center Stage

When
less isn't more and
you want desserts that will
make children crow with excitement
and make grown-ups *ooh!* and *aah!*, then
this is the chapter for you.

There are sweets here for every party and every special occasion, and they are easy enough for the novice baker and dessert maker to manage with aplomb. Any tea party would welcome cake platters piled high with Pinkalicious Princess Cupcakes—tender little white cakes tinted rosebud pink, topped with a fluffy pompadour of Pink Marshmallow Fluff Icing, and glammed up with pink coconut and edible glitter. Knickerbocker Glory Parfaits and Miraculous Mile-High Strawberry Fudge Ice-Cream Pie are wonderfully easy treats that incorporate the fruits of summer into delicious desserts children will love to help prepare—and eat. Play Willy Wonka and make edible party favors by dipping balloons in melted chocolate to create chocolate candy cups, then fill them with bites of Flufftastic Fudge, peanut butter bonbons, or big, fat homemade marshmallows dolled up and bejeweled like movie stars going to the Oscars, drizzled with brightly colored confectionery coating, sprinkles, and sugar flowers. Top off this chapter full of fun and fancy sweets with a big, old-fashioned chocolate birthday cake piled high with billows of the creamiest, dreamiest chocolate frosting ever. So plan a party and make a big, beautiful dessert—and watch your celebration sparkle.

Shortbread is one of the most versatile and forgiving cookies. You can dress it up or leave it starkly plain, and it is always delicious. Shortbread requires only one real, true thing: the very best butter. If you don't have butter, you don't have shortbread, no matter how much chocolate, nuts, or other extras you may stir in. Fresh, unsalted butter is the key to shortbread nirvana. Of course, I am fond of all those stirred-in frivolities, and I have stirred in plenty of them here, adding chunks of chocolate, a handful of nuts, and a judicious sprinkling of chopped English toffee. You really need the nuts for the proper craggy, mountain effect, but if there are die-hard nut haters in your midst, you can leave the nuts out completely or substitute raisins, dried cherries, or diced dried apricots instead.

Matterhorn Mountain Shortbread Cookies MAKES 22 TO 24 COOKIES

2¼ CUPS ALL-PURPOSE FLOUR

¼ TEASPOON BAKING POWDER

½ TEASPOON SALT

1 CUP (2 STICKS) UNSALTED BUTTER, AT ROOM TEMPERATURE

1 CUP CONFECTIONERS' SUGAR, SIFTED

1 TEASPOON PURE VANILLA EXTRACT

½ CUP SEMISWEET CHOCOLATE CHUNKS

½ CUP COARSELY CHOPPED TOASTED PECANS OR WALNUTS

3 CHOCOLATE-COVERED ENGLISH TOFFEE CANDY BARS LIKE HEATH BARS OR SKOR BAR (1.5 OUNCES EACH), COARSELY CHOPPED

4 OUNCES WHITE CHOCOLATE, MELTED

LINE 2 BAKING SHEETS WITH PARCHMENT PAPER.

IN A MEDIUM BOWL, sift together the flour, baking powder, and salt. Set aside.

IN A LARGE BOWL AND USING A HAND MIXER SET AT LOW SPEED, beat together the butter and confectioners' sugar until creamy, about 2 minutes. Beat in the vanilla. Sift the flour mixture over the butter mixture and beat together at very low speed just long enough to form a soft dough. With a large spatula, stir in the chocolate, nuts, and toffee bar chunks.

ROLL 2 HEAPING TABLESPOONS OF THE DOUGH INTO A BALL and place on one of the prepared baking sheets. Repeat with the remaining dough, placing the dough balls at least 2 inches apart. You should have 22 to 24 cookies. Refrigerate for at least 30 minutes to firm up slightly. (At this point, the shortbread dough can be refrigerated in a tightly covered container for up to 1 week.)

CONTINUED

I would rather eat shortbread than any cake or cookie in the world.
I would turn my back on a chocolate truffle or a banana split
for one piece of crisp, melting shortbread.
from Home Cooking, by Laurie Colwin

I'm Melting!

Melting white chocolate is a more delicate procedure than melting dark chocolate, and requires extra care. If it is heated at too high a temperature, or for too long, it will overheat and scorch, separating into clumps instead of melting smoothly. Start with finely chopped white chocolate. The more finely chopped the chocolate, the faster and easier it will melt. Place in a microwave-safe bowl (not plastic; try a glass or ceramic bowl). Melt for 30 seconds at half-power in the microwave. Remove from the microwave and stir until smooth. If the chocolate is not completely melted, return to the microwave for 15-second intervals until soft enough to stir smooth. Use immediately.

Matterhorn Mountain Shortbread Cookies
CONTINUED

PREHEAT THE OVEN TO 300°F.

BAKE UNTIL FIRM AND JUST BEGINNING TO TURN GOLDEN BROWN AROUND THE EDGES, and the cookies form a soft sloping mountain shape, 25 to 30 minutes. Remove from the oven and let cool completely on the baking sheets before removing.

WHEN COMPLETELY COOL, dip the tops of the cookies in the melted white chocolate. Let sit until the chocolate firms up completely. Serve, or store in a covered container for up to 1 week.

I still remember my third-grade Halloween party. So when my oldest daughter, Olivia, was in the third grade, I decided to throw her a party, too. I satisfied my inner Martha and draped the furniture in white sheets, and spent hours tea-dying ripped cheesecloth to hang as curtains. Olivia and I cut hundreds of bats from black construction paper and taped them all over the walls and ceiling. We laid a ghostly buffet with our scariest tarnished silver cake stands and platters and piled them high with chocolate bats, orange shortbread pumpkins, and these airy meringues. The scariest thing about the party was how exhausted we all were when it was over. These little ghosts have reappeared over the years—it's a great was to use up egg whites left over from making the Wicked Good Chocolate Peanut Butter Pudding Cups (page 57). They make a great nibble alongside a dollop of pudding, as you relax with your feet up waiting for the first trick-or-treaters to knock at your door.

Ghostly Meringues

MAKES ABOUT 2 DOZEN 4-INCH GHOSTS

6 EGG WHITES, AT ROOM TEMPERATURE

½ TEASPOON CREAM OF TARTAR

PINCH OF SALT

1 TEASPOON PURE VANILLA EXTRACT

1 CUP SUPERFINE SUGAR

1 CUP CONFECTIONERS' SUGAR, SIFTED

48 MINI SEMISWEET CHOCOLATE CHIPS (ABOUT ½ CUP)

SET A RACK IN THE MIDDLE SHELF OF THE OVEN AND PLACE A SECOND RACK ON THE TOP SHELF. Preheat the oven to 200°F. Line 2 baking sheets with parchment paper and set aside.

IN A LARGE METAL BOWL AND USING AN ELECTRIC MIXER SET AT LOW SPEED, beat the egg whites and cream of tartar until foamy. Add the salt, increase the mixer speed to medium-high, and continue beating until soft peaks form. Beat in the vanilla.

GRADUALLY, add the superfine sugar, 1 tablespoon at a time, beating until the meringue forms stiff, glossy peaks.

SIFT THE CONFECTIONERS' SUGAR, a second time, over the meringue. Using a rubber spatula, carefully fold the sugar into the meringue just until no streaks of sugar remain. Do not fold any more than is necessary, as overmixing will deflate the meringue.

SPOON THE MERINGUE INTO A LARGE SELF-SEALING PLASTIC BAG. Use a sharp pair of scissors to snip ½ inch off from one corner of the bag to form a makeshift piping bag.

CONTINUED

Meringue 101

Separate When Cold: Separating the yolk from the white is easiest when the egg is very cold. If a trace of yolk remains in the egg whites, they won't whip up properly.

Add a Little Acid: A little lemon juice or cream of tartar will help stabilize the egg whites and help them whip up higher and lighter and make them less likely to collapse.

Metal Bowls Are Best: A large stainless-steel bowl is the best choice when whipping egg whites. Plastic bowls are harder to keep clean and the smooth sides of ceramic make it harder for the meringue to cling together and form a tight structure.

Beat Them Well: Start beating the egg whites slowly. Look for soft, billowy mounds with well-defined peaks that form and gently fall over when the beaters are lifted. These are called soft peaks. Egg whites beaten to soft peaks won't cling to the sides of the bowl, but shift from side to side in one mass when the bowl is tilted. For crisp meringue cookies, like our Ghostly Meringues, the egg whites need to be beaten to stiff, glossy peaks. They will have a dense, creamy texture and the peaks will stand firmly upright when the beaters are lifted. They will cling to the bowl and be so firm they will not fall from the bowl if it is turned upside down. You will know your egg whites are overbeaten if they become dry and granular, eventually collapsing and separating.

Two Types of Sugar: Beating the egg whites with granulated sugar and folding sifted confectioners' sugar in before piping the meringue cookies ensures a meringue that is very crisp, very white, and very crunchy.

Ghostly Meringues

CONTINUED

"This is what clouds should taste like."
Sam Farnworth, age 10,
while making meringues

PIPE 12 MERINGUE GHOSTS ONTO EACH LINED BAKING SHEET: Hold the bag upright and squeeze the meringue, forming a wide base, a slightly smaller middle, and a curled tip (almost as if you were piping a soft-serve ice-cream cone) to form a chubby, upright ghost shape. Press two chocolate chips (flat side out) into the face of each ghost to form eyes.

BAKE THE MERINGUES FOR 2 HOURS, or until crisp. Baking the meringues for a long time at a low temperature ensures they will remain crisp and very white. If the meringues start to color, reduce the oven temperature to 175°F. When the meringues are crisp, turn the oven off and allow them to cool in the oven for at least 2 hours, but preferably overnight.

STORE THE MERINGUES IN A TIGHTLY COVERED CONTAINER FOR UP TO 1 WEEK.

These are truly, deeply, darkly, sticky, delicious chocolate cupcakes. If you are someone who, shockingly, thinks a dessert can be "too chocolaty," these may not be for you. The honey in the batter makes them supremely moist, and dense, but not heavy. They are hands-down the messiest cupcakes I have ever made and tried to eat in a dainty or tidy fashion. First of all, the desire to take large, unladylike bites is almost too difficult to overcome. They should be eaten outside in the playground, brought to birthday parties held at safe places like bowling alleys or amusement parks, or in the home of friends who don't mind crumbs and smears of chocolate on their furniture. Bless them.

Bumblebee Sting Cupcakes

MAKES 24 CUPCAKES

¾ CUP NATURAL COCOA POWDER

¾ CUP WARM WATER

½ CUP CANOLA OIL OR OTHER MILD VEGETABLE OIL

1 CUP MILD HONEY

2 LARGE EGGS

1 CUP BUTTERMILK

2 TEASPOONS PURE VANILLA EXTRACT

1 CUP GRANULATED SUGAR

2¼ CUPS ALL-PURPOSE FLOUR

2 TEASPOONS BAKING POWDER

½ TEASPOON BAKING SODA

½ TEASPOON SALT

CREAMY HONEY-CHOCOLATE FROSTING (FACING PAGE)

FONDANT BUMBLEBEES (PAGE 72)

SET A RACK IN THE MIDDLE OF THE OVEN AND PREHEAT THE OVEN TO 350°F. Line two 12-cup muffin pans with paper liners. (Dress your cupcakes in the ultimate dark chocolate couture by purchasing dark chocolate–brown paper liners—somehow your cupcakes will taste even more chocolaty presented this way!)

IN A VERY LARGE SAUCEPAN OVER MEDIUM HEAT, stir together the cocoa powder, water, oil, and honey. Stir just until the cocoa is dissolved and the mixture is combined and very smooth. Remove from the heat and whisk in the eggs, buttermilk, and vanilla.

SIFT THE SUGAR, flour, baking powder, baking soda, and salt into the chocolate mixture. Using an electric hand mixer set at medium-high speed, beat the wet and dry ingredients together just until combined, 1 to 2 minutes.

FILL EACH MUFFIN CUP TWO-THIRDS FULL WITH BATTER. Bake until a skewer inserted into the center of a cupcake comes out clean, 18 to 22 minutes. Let cool completely on a wire rack. Frost the cooled cupcakes with Creamy Honey-Chocolate Frosting and garnish with a fondant bee.

Creamy Honey-Chocolate Frosting

MAKES 3 TO 3½ CUPS

This honey-sweetened frosting was enthusiastically tested by Brownie Troop 5145. Future chocoholics among this group of 7-year-old girls licked their cupcake liners clean.

1 CUP SEMISWEET CHOCOLATE CHIPS

2 CUPS MILK CHOCOLATE CHIPS

1 CUP HEAVY CREAM

2 TABLESPOONS MILD HONEY

½ TEASPOON PURE VANILLA EXTRACT

COMBINE THE CHOCOLATE CHIPS IN A BOWL AND SET ASIDE. Combine the cream and honey in a saucepan and bring to a boil. Pour the honey mixture over the combined chocolates and let stand for 1 minute to soften the chocolate. Add the vanilla and stir together until very smooth. Let cool completely. Refrigerate until very thick but still spreadable, 2 to 3 hours. Alternatively, you can make this frosting the day before it is needed and leave it overnight, covered, at room temperature to firm up

Fondant Bumblebees

MAKES 24 BEES

Colored fondant is easy to find in craft stores like Michaels or through cake-decorating supply stores and confectionery sites online.

3 OUNCES YELLOW FONDANT

3 OUNCES CHOCOLATE-BROWN FONDANT

48 SLICED ALMONDS, PLUS MORE TO ALLOW FOR BREAKAGE

THERE ARE TWO WAYS TO MAKE FONDANT BEES:

(1) ROLL THE YELLOW FONDANT INTO A LONG ROPE. Do the same with the brown fondant. Twist the two ropes together and then gently roll the twisted rope with your hands on a flat work surface to form one smooth, marbled rope. Pinch bits of this marbled fondant into small, marble-size pieces and mold into ½-inch to ¾-inch bee-shaped lozenges. Stick 2 almonds into the body to form wings. Place the "bee" on the frosted cupcake. Chill until ready to serve. If you like, give each bee "eyes" by attaching two mini chocolate chips to the fondant (pressing the pointed side of the chip into the fondant), or roll tiny pieces of brown fondant into little balls, flatten, and stick these to the bees as eyes.

(2) BREAK OFF MARBLE-SIZE PIECES OF THE YELLOW FONDANT AND ROLL INTO SMOOTH BALLS. Roll small pieces of the brown fondant into very skinny ropes. Wrap 2 or 3 skinny ropes around the ball of yellow fondant and roll it on a flat surface to flatten the ropes and smooth into the yellow fondant and form a ¾- to 1-inch oval lozenge. Stick 2 almonds into the body to form wings. Add eyes to the bee as above.

FONDANT BUMBLEBEES CAN BE MADE UP TO 3 DAYS IN ADVANCE AND STORED IN A TIGHTLY covered container at room temperature.

I love the storybook *Pinkalicious*, about a little girl who eats too many of her favorite pink cupcakes until she develops an acute case of "pinkititus," and turns bright pink herself. The only cure is to eat green, green, green; from pickles and peas to olives and okra. The illustrations are quirky and divine, and the desire to create my own "pinkalicious" cupcake was a challenge I couldn't resist. For the pinkest cupcakes, search out bright pink cupcake liners and a variety of pink decorations from edible glitter, jimmies, sanding sugar, and sprinkles to doll them up. Forget restraint—the glitzier, the better. These cupcakes are very easy to make and are best served the day they are baked. If time is of the essence, you can make the pink frosting a day or two in advance, storing it in a tightly covered container in the refrigerator. Make sure you allow the frosting to come to room temperature before you start decorating the cupcakes.

Pinkalicious Princess Cupcakes MAKES 18 CUPCAKES

2¼ CUPS CAKE FLOUR

1 TABLESPOON BAKING POWDER

1½ CUPS GRANULATED SUGAR

1 TEASPOON SALT

½ CUP (1 STICK) UNSALTED BUTTER, AT ROOM TEMPERATURE, CUT INTO 8 PIECES

1 CUP WHOLE MILK, AT ROOM TEMPERATURE

1½ TEASPOONS PURE VANILLA EXTRACT

4 LARGE EGG WHITES, AT ROOM TEMPERATURE

PINK GEL FOOD COLORING

PINK MARSHMALLOW FLUFF ICING (PAGE 75)

PINK SANDING SUGAR, PINK JIMMIES, SPRINKLES, EDIBLE GLITTER, PINK-COLORED FLAKED COCONUT (SEE NOTE), AND PINK ROYAL ICING OR SUGAR FLOWERS FOR DECORATING

PREHEAT THE OVEN TO 350°F. Line two standard 12-cup muffin pans with eighteen pink paper liners, or make these jumbo Pinkalicious cupcakes and use large "Texas-size" muffin tins and liners (if using the larger pans, this recipe will make about 8 cupcakes).

IN A LARGE METAL MIXING BOWL, sift together the flour, baking powder, sugar, and salt. Add the butter and start to beat together using an electric mixer set at low speed. While you are beating, add the milk a little at a time, and continue beating for about 2 minutes. Slowly add the egg whites and vanilla to the batter and beat at high speed, scraping the bowl down occasionally, for 1 to 2 minutes. While you are beating, drop in 4 or 5 drops of pink or red food coloring to achieve your desired shade of pink.

FILL THE LINED MUFFIN CUPS ABOUT TWO-THIRDS FULL (about a heaping ¼ cup batter each). Bake just until a toothpick inserted into the center of a cupcake comes out clean, 18 to 20 minutes.

REMOVE FROM THE OVEN AND LET THE CUPCAKES COOL COMPLETELY ON A WIRE RACK. When completely cool, frost with Pink Marshmallow Fluff Icing. Mound a large dollop of the icing onto each cupcake with an icing spatula, or fill a piping bag fitted with a large star or round tip and pipe the icing onto each cupcake. Decorate with pink coconut and/or pink sanding sugar, or pink jimmies, pink sprinkles, and a good dose of edible pink glitter—and perhaps a pink sugar flower or two. Don't be shy, be glitzy and gaudy!

Egg Whites Only, Please!

Why does this recipe call for egg whites instead of whole eggs? Using only egg whites in a cake recipe yields a snow-white batter that will turn a delightful shade of pink when the food coloring is added. Also, cakes made with egg whites instead of whole eggs tend to be lighter and more delicate in flavor and texture—perfect for the most pinkalicious of cupcake treats.

Tinted Coconut: Add 1 or 2 drops of food coloring to a self-sealing plastic bag. Add 2 or 3 cups of sweetened flaked coconut and seal the bag. Shake the bag to distribute the color around the coconut until it is uniformly colored. Add more food coloring, one drop at a time, for a more intense shade of pink.

Let's make cupcakes! What color do you want?
"Pink!" I said. "Pink, pink, pink!"
from Pinkalicious, *by Victoria Kann and Elizabeth Kann*

Pink Marshmallow Fluff Icing

MAKES ABOUT 4 CUPS

This luscious icing is easy, sweet and fluffy—and very pretty in pink.

2 JARS (7½ OUNCES EACH) MARSHMALLOW FLUFF OR MARSHMALLOW CREAM

2 CUPS (4 STICKS) UNSALTED BUTTER, AT ROOM TEMPERATURE, EACH STICK CUT INTO 4 PIECES

3½ TO 4 CUPS CONFECTIONERS' SUGAR, SIFTED

1 TEASPOON PURE VANILLA EXTRACT

PINCH OF SALT

PINK GEL FOOD COLORING

SPOON THE MARSHMALLOW FLUFF INTO A LARGE BOWL. Using an electric mixer set at medium speed, start beating the marshmallow fluff, adding the butter one piece at a time, beating well between each addition. When the butter is completely incorporated, and the mixture is light and fluffy, beat in 3½ cups of the confectioners' sugar, the vanilla, and salt. Add the food coloring as you are beating the icing, 1 or 2 drops at a time, until the desired level of "pinkness" is achieved. I favor a lovely shade of cotton-candy pink. Taste the icing, and if a sweeter taste or slightly thicker texture is desired, beat in the additional ½ cup confectioners' sugar. Use immediately, or cover and refrigerate until ready to use. If refrigerating, remember to allow the frosting to come to room temperature before using. Do not overbeat the frosting after it comes to room temperature, or it will lose volume and become too soft to properly ice the cupcakes.

Tall ice cream sundaes layered with a variety of fruits and sauces are often called *parfaits*, which in French means "perfect." I think that moniker suits the Knickerbocker Glory well. This splendid confection was invented in the United Kingdom around the 1930s, and was always presented in the tall, classic parfait glass to show off its many layers of ice cream, fresh and brandied fruits, chocolate sauce, and sometimes even cubes of fruit gelatin. But where did the name come from? The colorful presentation of ice cream, fruit and syrups were said to resemble the once-popular long striped stockings called "knickerbockers." My version of this grand old dessert layers together a quick and easy blueberry sauce with vanilla ice cream and fresh sliced strawberries. I like to serve these patriotic parfaits on July 4th, topped with little paper flags of the Stars and Stripes and the Union Jack—tipping my hat to our friends "across the pond."

Knickerbocker Glory Parfaits

SERVES 4

2 CUPS FROZEN BLUEBERRIES

2 TABLESPOONS FRESH LEMON JUICE

1 TEASPOON LEMON ZEST

½ CUP GRANULATED SUGAR

1 CUP FRESH OR FROZEN BLUEBERRIES

2 PINTS STRAWBERRIES, SLICED

1 CUP HEAVY CREAM

3 TABLESPOONS CONFECTIONERS' SUGAR

½ TEASPOON PURE VANILLA EXTRACT

2 PINTS PREMIUM VANILLA ICE CREAM

4 MARASCHINO CHERRIES

RED, WHITE, AND BLUE SPRINKLES (SOMETIMES CALLED JIMMIES, OR VERMICELLI) FOR TOPPING

IN A MEDIUM SAUCEPAN OVER MEDIUM HEAT, combine the 2 cups frozen blueberries with the lemon juice, lemon zest, and ¼ cup of the granulated sugar. Cook until the berries start to pop and exude their juices. Cover the berries and simmer over medium-low heat until very soft, about 10 minutes. Remove from the heat and let cool slightly. Purée the berries until smooth. Toss the warm sauce with the 1 cup of fresh or frozen blueberries. Cover and refrigerate until ready to use.

ABOUT 30 MINUTES BEFORE SERVING, toss the sliced strawberries with the remaining ¼ cup granulated sugar. Set aside to macerate.

IN A LARGE BOWL, combine the cream, confectioners' sugar, and vanilla. Using an electric mixer set at medium speed, beat until the mixture thickens and forms soft peaks when the beaters are lifted. Chill until ready to top the sundaes.

IN A TALL, clear sundae glass, spoon in 1 or 2 tablespoons of the blueberry sauce. Continue to layer ice cream, blueberry sauce, and sliced strawberries for a patriotic parfait. Top with a large dollop of the whipped cream, a maraschino cherry, and red, white, and blue jimmies. Serve immediately.

The idea of making your own candy may seem daunting, but everyone can make a delicious pan of fudge with the magical addition of Marshmallow Fluff. Folding part of the Marshmallow Fluff in at the end gives this fudge a lighter, fluffier texture.

Flufftastic Fudge

MAKES 5 POUNDS

12 OUNCES SEMISWEET CHOCOLATE CHIPS

12 OUNCES MILK CHOCOLATE CHIPS

1 TEASPOON PURE VANILLA EXTRACT

8 TABLESPOONS (1 STICK) UNSALTED BUTTER, PLUS MORE FOR BUTTERING THE PAN

4 ½ CUPS GRANULATED SUGAR

1 LARGE CAN (12 OUNCES) EVAPORATED WHOLE MILK

1 TEASPOON SALT

2 JARS (7 ½ OUNCES EACH) MARSHMALLOW FLUFF

2 CUPS CHOPPED WALNUTS, TOASTED AND COOLED (OPTIONAL)

LIGHTLY BUTTER A 9-BY-13-INCH PAN. Set aside.

IN A LARGE HEATPROOF BOWL, combine the semisweet chocolate chips, milk chocolate chips, vanilla, and 4 tablespoons of the butter (cut into small pieces). Set aside.

IN A VERY LARGE SAUCEPAN OR DUTCH OVEN OVER LOW HEAT, combine the sugar, milk, the remaining 4 tablespoons butter, and the salt. Stir until the butter is melted and the sugar is dissolved. Increase the heat to medium-high and bring to a boil, stirring constantly. When the mixture starts to boil, add 1 jar of the Marshmallow Fluff and stir until the marshmallow has melted into the hot milk mixture. Return the mixture to a full boil. Boil vigorously, stirring constantly, until the mixture registers 234°F on a candy thermometer, or forms a soft ball when a little is dropped into a glass of ice water, about 6 minutes.

IMMEDIATELY POUR THE HOT SUGAR MIXTURE OVER THE INGREDIENTS IN THE BOWL AND FOLD together just until the chocolate and the butter are melted. Fold the remaining jar of Marshmallow Fluff and the walnuts (if using) into the fudge, just until combined, and then pour the mixture into the prepared pan. Let the fudge cool completely before cutting it into squares.

FUDGE WILL KEEP, tightly covered, for up to 1 week.

When I was 20, I got my first paying job as a cook. I was the lunch cook for a small family resort high in the Trinity Alps of California. Every Friday was the dinner cook's day off, so that day I was responsible for lunch and dinner. Really, it should not have been that difficult, as the guests cooked their own steaks every Friday night on the huge outdoor grill and all I had to do was come up with a few savory side dishes and a killer dessert. My first night was a disaster. My sautéed mushrooms were overcooked, sadly shriveled, and underseasoned, and my attempts at hashbrown potatoes were simultaneously raw, greasy, and burnt. In a full-scale panic, I prayed dessert would save me. Earlier in the day I had puréed strawberries, blended them with vanilla ice cream, and piled it all sky-high on a crisp coconut crust. When I served hefty wedges of this pie I could practically hear the heavens break open and the angels sing—the ice cream tasted miraculously fresh, like homemade strawberry ice cream, and it was a beautiful thing to behold, smothered in fudge sauce and whipped cream. I saved my job, and I have depended on dessert to save me ever since. In the version here, I have substituted a chocolate cookie crust to please more palates, but the method, and the magic, remains the same.

Miraculous Mile-High Strawberry Fudge Ice-Cream Pie

SERVES 6 TO 8

ONE 9-INCH CHOCOLATE COOKIE CRUST (FACING PAGE)

EASY-AS-PIE HOT FUDGE SAUCE (FACING PAGE)

1 POUND FROZEN UNSWEETENED STRAWBERRIES

¼ CUP GRANULATED SUGAR

4 PINTS PREMIUM VANILLA ICE CREAM

2 CUPS HEAVY CREAM

⅓ CUP CONFECTIONERS' SUGAR, SIFTED

1 TEASPOON PURE VANILLA EXTRACT

8 LARGE FRESH STRAWBERRIES

COVER THE BOTTOM OF THE COOLED CHOCOLATE COOKIE CRUST WITH ABOUT ½ CUP Easy-as-Pie Hot Fudge Sauce. Set aside.

ALLOW THE STRAWBERRIES TO THAW COMPLETELY. Spoon the thawed berries and any accumulated juices into a blender or food processor with the granulated sugar and blend until very smooth. You should have 2 to 2½ cups of strawberry purée.

REMOVE THE PINTS OF ICE CREAM FROM THE FREEZER AND DO NOT ALLOW THEM TO SOFTEN. Cut the cartons from the ice cream using a sharp knife or scissors so that the ice cream remains very firm. Cut each unwrapped pint of ice cream into four large pieces. Place the ice cream in the metal mixing bowl of a stand mixer. Fit the mixer with the paddle attachment and, with the mixer set at low speed, start blending the ice cream with the strawberry purée. Increase mixer speed to medium high and continue drizzling the purée into the ice cream a little at a time. Mix until the ice cream is creamy and the strawberry sauce is fully incorporated, but the mixture is still fairly firm and the ice cream is not melted. Immediately spoon the ice cream into the prepared pie shell, mounding it high. Cover the surface of the ice cream with plastic wrap and store the pie in the freezer for at least 5 hours, and preferably overnight, before serving.

JUST BEFORE SERVING, using an electric mixer set at medium speed, beat the cream, confectioners' sugar, and vanilla together until soft peaks form.

REMOVE THE PIE FROM THE FREEZER. It is easiest to cut this large pie if it is first removed from the pie pan; run a knife around the edge of the crust and carefully tip the pie out of the pan onto a cutting board. Using a very large chef's knife, slice the pie in half. Cut each half into 3 or 4 wedges. Place each wedge of pie on a dessert plate. Drizzle each serving with hot fudge sauce and top with a very large dollop of the whipped cream. Garnish each slice of pie with a fresh strawberry, and serve.

Chocolate Cookie Crust

MAKES ONE 9-INCH PIE CRUST

25 TO 28 CHOCOLATE SANDWICH COOKIES (LIKE OREOS)

5 TABLESPOONS UNSALTED BUTTER, MELTED

SET A RACK IN THE MIDDLE OF THE OVEN AND PREHEAT THE OVEN TO 350°F.

IN A FOOD PROCESSOR FITTED WITH A STAINLESS-STEEL BLADE, process the cookies, cream filling included, until they are crushed into fine crumbs. Measure 2½ cups cookie crumbs and mix with the melted butter.

LIGHTLY COAT A 9-INCH PYREX PIE PLATE (I find the pie is easier to remove from a Pyrex pan) with nonstick cooking spray. Press the cookie mixture firmly and evenly into the bottom and up the sides of the pie pan. Bake the crust until lightly crisp and fragrant, 6 to 8 minutes. Let cool completely before filling.

Easy-as-Pie Hot Fudge Sauce

MAKES 2 CUPS

8 OUNCES FINELY CHOPPED SEMISWEET CHOCOLATE OR CHOCOLATE CHIPS

1 CUP HEAVY CREAM

4 TABLESPOONS LIGHT CORN SYRUP

1 TEASPOON PURE VANILLA EXTRACT

PLACE THE CHOCOLATE IN A BOWL.

IN A LARGE SAUCEPAN OVER HIGH HEAT, bring the cream and corn syrup to a boil. Pour over the chocolate and allow it to sit for 2 minutes. Stir until the chocolate is melted and the mixture is smooth. Stir in the vanilla.

Every cook needs a foolproof, perfectly simple, and simply delicious chocolate cake to pull out for special occasions. This cake definitely fills the bill. It is very moist and fudgy, but still tender. This cake will make any occasion feel special when it is piled high with a luscious and creamy frosting that tastes just like melted chocolate bars. It would be equally lovely decked out in a fluffy swath of whipped cream, or iced with the Pink Marshmallow Fluff Icing (page 75). Any way you choose to decorate it, this cake is a winner.

The Best Chocolate Birthday Cake Ever SERVES 8

¾ CUP NATURAL COCOA POWDER

1 CUP BOILING WATER

¾ CUP SOUR CREAM

1 CUP (2 STICKS) UNSALTED BUTTER, AT ROOM TEMPERATURE

1½ CUPS GRANULATED SUGAR

½ CUP FIRMLY PACKED LIGHT BROWN SUGAR

2 LARGE EGGS, AT ROOM TEMPERATURE

1½ TEASPOONS PURE VANILLA EXTRACT

1¾ CUPS ALL-PURPOSE FLOUR

1 TEASPOON BAKING POWDER

1 TEASPOON BAKING SODA

½ TEASPOON SALT

MELT-IN-YOUR-MOUTH CHOCOLATE FROSTING (FACING PAGE)

PREHEAT THE OVEN TO 350°F. Coat two 9-inch round cake pans with nonstick spray and line with parchment paper rounds. Set aside.

SIFT THE COCOA POWDER INTO A SMALL BOWL AND STIR IN THE BOILING WATER TO DISSOLVE and make the cocoa "bloom." Whisk together until completely smooth. Let cool completely, and then whisk the sour cream into the cocoa mixture.

IN A LARGE BOWL, beat the butter and sugars together with an electric hand mixer set on medium speed until light and fluffy, about 4 minutes. Beat in the eggs one at a time, then beat in the cooled cocoa mixture and the vanilla.

SIFT THE FLOUR, baking powder, baking soda, and salt over the batter and fold in gently, using a rubber spatula, until the flour is completely combined into the batter.

DIVIDE THE BATTER BETWEEN THE TWO PREPARED PANS AND SPREAD EVENLY. Bake until a toothpick or cake tester inserted into the center of the cake comes out clean, 25 to 30 minutes. Transfer to a wire rack and let cool completely.

TO FROST, invert one layer onto a cake plate, and remove the parchment circle. Spread 1 cup of frosting over the surface of the cake. Invert the second layer over the first, and remove the parchment paper. Frost the top and sides of the cake with the remaining icing.

What does it mean to make cocoa "bloom?"

Cocoa adds a deep, intense chocolate flavor to cakes. In order to help the cocoa reach its maximum flavor potential, dissolve the cocoa in warm water. The added water also contributes moisture to the cake batter, making the texture velvety and tender.

Cake Life Insurance: Lining layer cake pans with parchment paper is my version of cake life insurance—you never know when you might need it, so use it every time you bake to make sure your cake layers release cleanly from their pans. Trace the bottom of the cake pan onto parchment paper. Cut the circle out with scissors. Coat the bottom and sides of the cake pan lightly with nonstick cooking spray and fit the paper circle into the bottom of the pan. Coat the paper very lightly with nonstick spray and fill the pan with the cake batter. To release the baked cake layer without it sticking, run a thin bladed knife around the edge of the cake and invert onto a wire rack or cake plate. Peel away the parchment paper and discard before frosting the cake.

Melt-In-Your-Mouth Chocolate Frosting

MAKES 3½ CUPS

This frosting is buttery and flavorful with lots of body without being gritty or too sweet. It spreads beautifully and is perfect for this rich, fudgy cake or as a frosting for cupcakes.

1 CUP SEMISWEET CHOCOLATE CHIPS

1 CUP MILK CHOCOLATE CHIPS

½ CUP (1 STICK) UNSALTED BUTTER, CUT INTO 8 PIECES

1 CUP SOUR CREAM

1 TEASPOON PURE VANILLA EXTRACT

LARGE PINCH OF SALT

1 POUND CONFECTIONERS' SUGAR, SIFTED

IN A LARGE MICROWAVE-SAFE BOWL, combine the semisweet and milk chocolate chips with the butter. Heat on high for 1 minute. Stir the mixture together. If the butter is not completely melted and the chocolate chips do not easily stir smooth, heat again at 15-second intervals, stirring until smooth. Using a hand mixer set at low speed, beat in the sour cream, vanilla, and salt. Gradually add the confectioners' sugar until the frosting is smooth and spreadable.

"Oh, yes," said mother, "you may be sure that there will always be plenty of chocolate cake around here."
from A Baby Sister for Frances, *by Russell Hoban*

These eye-popping beauties just scream "I'm ready for my close-up, Mr. DeMille!" and like your favorite movie star, they are gorgeous and glamorous on the outside, and airy fluff (with no nutritional value) within. Homemade marshmallows are great fun to make, and a wonderful science project to discover what a little sugar, water, and gelatin can create. I like to make my marshmallows big and fat, just right for over-the-top embellishments. Dip or drizzle the marshmallows with melted, brightly colored confectionery coating, sprinkle with shimmering sanding sugar, coat them in jimmies and small candies, or give them funny faces by attaching googly eyes made from royal icing. You can even give your marshmallows the red-carpet treatment by brushing them with Luster Dust. (Beloved by cake decorators, luster dust is a glittering, shimmering powdered food coloring that comes in little pots like eye shadow.) You can leave the marshmallows their natural creamy color, or tint them pale lavender, pink, green, turquoise, or yellow, before cutting them into squares and dolling them up. Decorating homemade marshmallows is a fun birthday party activity, and party guests can take home small cellophane bags of their miniature masterpieces as favors, and as an edible reminder of their artistic and creative skill.

Glamorous Movie Star Marshmallows MAKES 25 BIG, FAT MARSHMALLOWS

CORNSTARCH FOR DUSTING

1 CUP COLD WATER

3 TABLESPOONS UNFLAVORED GRANULATED GELATIN

2 CUPS GRANULATED SUGAR

¾ CUP LIGHT CORN SYRUP

¼ TEASPOON SALT

1 TABLESPOON PURE VANILLA EXTRACT

CONFECTIONERS' SUGAR FOR DUSTING

CONFECTIONERY COATING (SOMETIMES CALLED "SUMMER COATING" OR "WAFER CHOCOLATE") IN VARIOUS COLORS, SANDING SUGAR, SPRINKLES, ROYAL ICING FLOWERS AND ROYAL ICING GOOGLY EYES, NONPAREILS, JIMMIES, MINI-CHOCOLATE CHIPS, MINI CANDIES (SEE SOURCES) FOR DECORATING

SPRAY A 9-BY-9-INCH PAN WITH NONSTICK COOKING SPRAY AND GENEROUSLY DUST WITH cornstarch. Set aside.

POUR ½ CUP OF THE COLD WATER INTO THE BOWL OF A STAND MIXER. Sprinkle the gelatin evenly over the water and allow the gelatin to sit and absorb the water, about 45 minutes.

IN A LARGE SAUCEPAN OVER MEDIUM HEAT, combine the remaining ½ cup water with the granulated sugar, corn syrup, and salt. Heat, swirling the pan occasionally, until the sugar dissolves. Increase the heat to high and let the mixture come to a boil. Cook the syrup, without stirring, until it reaches 240°F on a candy thermometer. Do not allow the syrup to go past 244°F or the marshmallows will be rubbery rather than tender. Remove the syrup from the heat and slowly beat it into the dissolved gelatin, using the whisk attachment of the mixer, set at low speed. After the syrup is added, increase the mixer speed to high and continue beating until the mixture is very thick and white but still warm, about 15 minutes. Beat in the vanilla.

CONTINUED

Glamorous Movie Star Marshmallows

CONTINUED

POUR THE MARSHMALLOW MIXTURE ONTO THE PREPARED PAN, smooth the top with a spatula, and dust liberally with confectioners' sugar. Let the marshmallow stand, uncovered, for 8 to 12 hours to firm up and "cure." Turn the marshmallow from the pan and brush off all the residual cornstarch. Place the marshmallow slab on a sheet of parchment paper dusted lightly with confectioners' sugar.

USING A LONG, sharp knife or pizza cutter, cut the slab of marshmallow into 5 even strips. Cut each strip into 5 square marshmallows. Roll each marshmallow in confectioners' sugar to coat the sticky edges. Shake, or brush off, any excess sugar. Store the marshmallows in a tightly covered container until ready to use.

WHEN READY TO DECORATE, set out small bowls filled with whatever variety of sanding sugar, sprinkles, jimmies, small candies, mini chocolate chips, royal icing flowers, or googly eyes you desire.

TO MELT THE CONFECTIONERY COATING, place about 2 cups of the wafers in a single layer on a microwave-safe dinner plate. Microwave at half-power for 1 minute. When properly heated the wafers will not lose their shape, but will look soft and shiny, and must be stirred smooth. Be careful not to overheat the coating, as it may "seize," which means it will thicken and turn hard and crumbly and you will not be able to remelt it.

Marshmallows: A History

Marshmallows are pure fun. Can you remember a time without marshmallows? With their chubby snow-white bodies and their soft, spongy middles, marshmallows star in many iconic American treats: roasted on sticks over a campfire, melted into milk chocolate and squished between two graham crackers; dotted over a casserole of sweet potatoes; melted and stirred into Rice Krispies for a favorite bake-sale treat. Despite their jet-puffed appearance, marshmallows have been around since the Egyptians began making them from the gooey sap of the marshmallow plant as early as 2000 BC. Marshmallows are so popular in the United States that we purchase around 90 million pounds of them per year. In Ligonier, Indiana, the self-named marshmallow capital of the world, a marshmallow festival is held at the end of every summer to celebrate this mighty puff.

USING A RUBBER SPATULA, transfer the melted confectionery coating to a small bowl for dipping and drizzling. To custom-color white confectionery coating, be sure to use a concentrated oil-based food coloring made specifically for candy-making (available at craft, candy-making, and cake decorating stores).

DRIZZLE AND DIP THE MARSHMALLOWS IN A VARIETY OF COLORFUL CONFECTIONERY COATINGS, and while still wet, sprinkle with sugars and sprinkles to decorate. Place the decorated marshmallows on a sheet of parchment paper or waxed paper and allow to dry—this should only take a few minutes. When set, the marshmallows can also be brushed with Luster Dust to make them glitter; use a new (unused) small paintbrush to lightly dust the coated marshmallows with gold, silver, or other shimmering colors. The marshmallows can be eaten or packed in small boxes or bags for later consumption. Although they will last awhile, homemade marshmallows taste their best when eaten within 2 or 3 days.

NOTE: A stand mixer like a KitchenAid is really a necessity when making these marshmallows. They require a lot of heavy-duty beating!

This chocolate tart may look sleek and dinner-party elegant, but don't let that fool you; the flavor will delight chocolate lovers of all ages, no matter how picky. The chocolate cookie crust is simple and quick and the filling is a slightly richer, glam version of the Wicked Good Chocolate Peanut Butter Pudding Cups (page 57). As with all of my favorite desserts, this one is best made a day in advance of serving, and its swanky good looks will charm the most discerning palates—toddler and gourmet alike.

Tuxedo Tart

SERVES 8

¼ CUP CORNSTARCH

1 CUP GRANULATED SUGAR

¼ TEASPOON SALT

5 TABLESPOONS DUTCH-PROCESSED COCOA POWDER

3 CUPS HALF-AND-HALF

6 LARGE EGG YOLKS

2 TEASPOONS PURE VANILLA EXTRACT

2 TABLESPOONS UNSALTED BUTTER

1 CUP SEMISWEET CHOCOLATE CHIPS

ONE 9-INCH CHOCOLATE COOKIE CRUST (FACING PAGE)

SWEETENED WHIPPED CREAM (FACING PAGE)

EASY WHITE CHOCOLATE CURLS (FACING PAGE) OR WHITE CHOCOLATE VERMICELLI FOR SPRINKLING (SEE SOURCES)

INTO A MEDIUM SAUCEPAN, sift together the cornstarch, sugar, salt, and cocoa powder. Slowly whisk in the half-and-half until the mixture is combined and smooth. Whisk in the egg yolks, one at a time, until smooth.

COOK THE MIXTURE OVER MEDIUM HEAT, whisking continuously, until it starts to thicken and large bubbles form and plop on the surface of the pudding like slowly boiling lava. Reduce the heat to low, and continue cooking, stirring continuously, for 1 minute. To check the consistency of the pudding, run your finger over the back of the stirring spoon; when it leaves a clean trail that does not fill in when you pull your finger away, it is thick enough.

REMOVE THE PUDDING FROM THE HEAT AND POUR THROUGH A FINE-MESH SIEVE PLACED OVER a clean bowl. Whisk the vanilla, butter, and chocolate chips into the strained pudding until thoroughly melted and combined. Carefully pour the mixture into the prepared pie crust, giving the filling a small shake if necessary to flatten it. Refrigerate the tart for at least 5 to 6 hours, or overnight, until it is cold and very firm.

TO SERVE, remove the side of the tart pan and place it on a serving platter. Lightly mound the whipped cream over the surface of the tart. Sprinkle the cream with Easy White Chocolate Curls or white chocolate vermicelli.

TO CUT THE TART, run a sharp knife under very hot water, wipe dry, and slice into slender wedges. Rinse the knife under hot water before cutting each slice, for clean wedges.

Chocolate Cookie Crust

MAKES ONE 9-INCH PIE CRUST

25 TO 30 CHOCOLATE SANDWICH
COOKIES (LIKE OREOS)

5 TABLESPOONS UNSALTED BUTTER,
MELTED

SET A RACK IN THE MIDDLE OF THE OVEN AND PREHEAT THE OVEN TO 350°F.

IN A FOOD PROCESSOR FITTED WITH A STAINLESS-STEEL BLADE, crush the cookies, cream filling included, until they are fine crumbs. Measure 2 cups of the crumbs and combine with the melted butter until the crumbs are thoroughly moistened. Press the crumb mixture firmly into the bottom and up the sides of a 9-inch or 10-inch tart pan with a removable bottom.

BAKE UNTIL LIGHTLY CRISP AND FRAGRANT, 6 to 8 minutes. Let cool completely before filling.

Sweetened Whipped Cream

MAKES 4 CUPS

2 CUPS HEAVY CREAM

½ CUP CONFECTIONERS' SUGAR

1 TEASPOON PURE VANILLA EXTRACT

CHILL A MIXING BOWL AND BEATERS IN THE FREEZER FOR 15 MINUTES (cream whips faster when the utensils are chilled). Combine the cream, sugar, and vanilla in the bowl and beat, using an electric mixer set at medium-low speed, until the cream starts to thicken. Increase the speed to medium-high and continue beating until it nearly doubles in volume and forms firm peaks.

Easy White Chocolate Curls

FOR SUPERQUICK CHOCOLATE CURLS, soften a thick chunk of white chocolate (about 6 ounces) in the microwave for 6 to 8 seconds. Scrape a vegetable peeler firmly down one side of the chocolate block to form a curl. Place the curls on a plate and refrigerate them until firm enough to handle.

These little cups are always popular and make great dessert or candy cups for parties. They are fun to make, and are an easy (if messy) project for children to help with. Be careful not to let the chocolate get too hot—not only might it thicken and seize (which means it will thicken and turn hard and crumbly, and you will not be able to remelt it, but will have to start all over again with fresh chocolate), making it impossible to dip the balloons, but the heat of the chocolate could make the balloons pop. Melting the chocolate on a plate in the microwave and transferring it to a bowl before you start dipping should eliminate this possible element of excitement.

Chocolate Balloon Cups

MAKES 6 TO 8 CHOCOLATE CUPS

6 TO 8 SMALL ROUND BALLOONS

1½ POUNDS FINELY CHOPPED SEMISWEET CHOCOLATE, WHITE CHOCOLATE, OR COLORED CONFECTIONERY COATING

BLOW UP THE BALLOONS UNTIL THEY ARE 3 TO 4 INCHES HIGH AND 5 TO 6 INCHES IN DIAMETER (the size of your balloons is really a personal preference, depending on what, and how much, you want to put in the cups). Knot the balloons and rinse under cold water. Dry thoroughly. Coat each balloon very lightly with nonstick cooking spray. Set aside.

PLACE 12 OUNCES OF THE CHOPPED CHOCOLATE IN A SINGLE LAYER ON A MICROWAVE-SAFE dinner plate. Place the plate, uncovered, in the microwave and heat at half-power for 1 minute. When heated, the chocolate will soften and look shiny, but will not completely lose its shape, and must be stirred smooth. Don't overheat the chocolate or let it come into contact with any water (not even a drop or two!), or it may seize. Scrape the melted chocolate into a bowl just large enough to accommodate the balloons.

LINE A BAKING SHEET WITH PARCHMENT PAPER. Spoon a teaspoon of melted chocolate onto the prepared baking sheet to form a base for the cup. Hold a balloon by the knotted end and dip and roll the balloon in the melted chocolate until it is evenly coated and reaches about halfway up the sides of the balloon. Hold the balloon upright over the bowl and allow any excess chocolate to drip off. Position the balloon firmly, standing upright, on the dollop of chocolate on the baking sheet. Hold the balloon steady until it can stand firmly on its own. Repeat with the remaining balloons, melting more chocolate as needed. Place the balloons in the refrigerator to harden. Refrigerate until very hard, 1 to 2 hours.

"Candy. That's what you have to eat for dinner every night when you're a pea. Candy. Candy. Candy."
from Little Pea, *by Amy Krouse Rosenthal*

TO REMOVE THE BALLOONS, grasp the knot firmly and pierce the balloon with a pin. Hang on to the balloon and carefully pull the deflating balloon away from the sides of the chocolate cup. Do not pull the balloon away from the chocolate too quickly or it may crack or break the cups. Discard balloons. At this point, you can fill the cup with fresh fruit and whipped cream, pudding, ice cream, or use it as an edible candy-cup and fill with squares of fudge, peanut butter bonbons, or other small candies. When the chocolate cups are ready, you can dress them up by drizzling the inside and/or the outside of the prepared cup with a contrasting color of melted chocolate. For example, drizzle a dark chocolate cup with melted white chocolate or pink confectionery coating and sprinkle with colored jimmies, sprinkles, or sanding sugar, if you like.

If you love peanut butter in your chocolate, and chocolate in your peanut butter, these baby bonbons were born just for you. Sweet and creamy, with a savory, crunchy kick from crushed pretzels and a lively crackle from bits of chopped English toffee, these candies will knock your socks off. They have been sampled by hungry elementary school teachers, skeptical culinary students, and little kids at the park, and everywhere they went these fat little bonbons were met with astonished delight at how tasty they were—and you will be amazed at how easy they are to create in your own kitchen.

Peanut Butter–Pretzel Bonbons

MAKES 35 TO 40 BONBONS

½ CUP (1 STICK) UNSALTED BUTTER, AT ROOM TEMPERATURE

2 CUPS CONFECTIONERS' SUGAR, SIFTED

2 CUPS CREAMY PEANUT BUTTER

2 CUPS (ABOUT 10 OUNCES) FINELY CHOPPED PRETZEL STICKS

1 CUP CRUSHED HEATH ENGLISH TOFFEE BITS, OR HEATH ALMOND BRICKLE BITS

1½ POUNDS FINELY CHOPPED SEMISWEET CHOCOLATE MELTED WITH 4 TABLESPOONS VEGETABLE SHORTENING, OR 1½ POUNDS DARK CHOCOLATE CONFECTIONERY COATING, MELTED, OR 2 TUBS (7 OUNCES EACH) DIPPING CHOCOLATE

1 CUP FINELY CHOPPED SALTED PEANUTS FOR ROLLING (OPTIONAL)

1 CUP BELGIAN CHOCOLATE JIMMIES (OR VERMICELLI) FOR ROLLING (OPTIONAL)

"These bonbons explode with yummy-ness."
Elise Marchessault, age 8, while eating her own peanut butter creations

IN A LARGE BOWL, using a hand-held electric mixer set at medium speed, beat together the butter and sugar until light and fluffy, about 2 minutes. Beat in the peanut butter until combined. Using a large rubber spatula, fold in the chopped pretzel sticks and toffee bits.

COVER AND REFRIGERATE THE MIXTURE UNTIL IT IS VERY FIRM, 2 to 3 hours. Roll the mixture, by heaping tablespoons, into 1-inch balls. Place on a parchment paper–lined baking sheet. Cover the bonbons with plastic wrap and freeze until they are very firm, about 30 minutes.

COMBINE THE CHOPPED CHOCOLATE AND SHORTENING, cut into small bits, on a large, microwave-safe dinner plate. Microwave at half-power for 1 minute. When melted, the chocolate will appear soft and shiny but will still hold its shape, stir smooth. If the chocolate is not completely melted, heat in 30-second increments, stirring until smooth. Transfer the chocolate to a medium bowl. If using confectionery coating, repeat this process without using the shortening. If using dipping chocolate in a tub, follow the dipping directions on the container.

TO MAKE DIPPING THE BONBONS EASY, and less messy, try wearing latex gloves, available in most pharmacies. Working with one bonbon at a time, quickly dip it in the melted chocolate, rolling it around to coat it completely. Rest the bonbon on a fork and let any excess chocolate drain away. Immediately roll the bonbon in the chopped peanuts (if using) or chocolate jimmies (if using) and place on the parchment-lined baking sheet to harden.

ALTERNATIVELY, place the dipped bonbon without the jimmies or nut coating, on the parchment-lined baking sheet and top with one perfect salted peanut or a sprinkling of crushed English toffee, or when the bonbon is firm, drizzle lightly with melted white chocolate.

THE BAKER'S CATALOGUE AT KING ARTHUR FLOUR

58 Billings Farm Road
White River Junction, VT 05051
800-827-6836
www.bakerscatalogue.com

Baking equipment and pans, Dutch-processed and natural cocoa, chocolates, confectionery coating, specialty flours, premium vanilla extract, chocolate jimmies and other baking supplies

CONFECTIONERY HOUSE

975 Hoosick Road
Troy, NY 12180
518-279-4245 or 518-279-3179
www.confectioneryhouse.com

Chocolate brown, blue, fuchsia, orange, yellow, purple, and green paper candy and cupcake liners and cake-decorating and candy-making supplies

DO IT WITH ICING

7240 Clairemont Mesa Boulevard
San Diego, CA 92111
858-268-1234
858-268-7991 (Fax)
www.doitwithicing.com

I couldn't fail to mention my favorite little mom-and-pop confectionery mecca here in San Diego. Owner Linda Bill carries a unique and varied selection of Luster Dust dried food coloring, gel and paste food coloring, sugar flowers, fondant, chocolate, bulk caramel, confectionery coating, sprinkles, real Belgian chocolate jimmies, and other baking, cake-decorating, and candy-making supplies

DURKEE-MOWER, INC.

P.O. Box 470
Lynn, MA 01903
781-593-8007
www.marshmallowfluff.com

Marshmallow Fluff and other fun Fluff products

MICHAELS STORES, INC.

8000 Bent Branch Drive
Irving, TX 75063
1-800-MICHAELS
www.michaels.com

Wilton baking products, baking pans, tart pans, Wilton "Candy-Melts" confectionery coating, food coloring, paper candy and cupcake liners, and other cake-decorating supplies

NEW YORK CAKE SUPPLIES

56 West 22nd Street
New York, NY 10010
212-675-CAKE
www.nycake.com

Cake pans, muffin pans, assorted tart pans, cake-decorating supplies, pastry bags and tips

PENZEYS SPICES

19300 West Janacek Court
P.O. Box 924
Brookfield, WI 53008-0924
262-785-7676
www.penzeys.com

Spices, whole vanilla beans, and double-strength vanilla extract

SWEET CELEBRATIONS

P.O. Box 39426
Edina, MN 55439-0426
800-328-6722
www.sweet.com

Bakeware, cake-decorating and candy-making supplies, confectionery coating, food coloring

WILLIAMS-SONOMA, INC.

Mail Order Department
P.O. Box 7456
San Francisco, CA 94102-7456
800-541-2233
www.williams-sonoma.com

KitchenAid mixers, food processors, hand mixers, knives, top-quality baking pans, baking sheets, tart pans, measuring cups, spoons, whisks, and anything your kitchen may need, including European chocolates and cocoa powders, vanilla beans, and raw sugars

INDEX

Table of Equivalents

The exact equivalents in the following tables have been rounded for convenience.

LENGTHS

U.S.	METRIC
1/8 inch	3 millimeters
1/4 inch	6 millimeters
1/2 inch	12 millimeters
1 inch	2.5 centimeters

LIQUID/DRY MEASUREMENTS

U.S.	METRIC
1/4 teaspoon	1.25 milliliters
1/2 teaspoon	2.5 milliliters
1 teaspoon	5 milliliters
1 tablespoon (3 teaspoons)	15 milliliters
1 fluid ounce (2 tablespoons)	30 milliliters
1/4 cup	60 milliliters
1/3 cup	80 milliliters
1/2 cup	120 milliliters
1 cup	240 milliliters
1 pint (2 cups)	480 milliliters
1 quart (4 cups, 32 ounces)	960 milliliters
1 gallon (4 quarts)	3.84 liters
1 ounce (by weight)	28 grams
1 pound	448 grams
2.2 pounds	1 kilogram

OVEN TEMPERATURE

FAHRENHEIT	CELSIUS	GAS
250	120	1/2
275	140	1
300	150	2
325	160	3
350	180	4
375	190	5
400	200	6
425	220	7
450	230	8
475	240	9
500	260	10